FUTURE INTRO

English for Work, Life, and Academic Success

Second Edition

Series Consultants
Sarah Lynn
Ronna Magy
Federico Salas-Isnardi

Authors
Yvonne Wong Nishio
with Jamie Greene,
Hilary Hodge,
Jessica Miller-Smith,
and Julie Schmidt

Pearson

Future Intro
English for Work, Life, and Academic Success

Copyright © 2021 by Pearson Education, Inc.

Pearson Education, 221 River Street, Hoboken, NJ 07030 USA

Staff credits: The people who made up the **Future** team, representing content development, design, manufacturing, marketing, multimedia, project management, publishing, rights management, and testing, are Pietro Alongi, Jennifer Castro, Dave Dickey, Gina DiLillo, Warren Fischbach, Pamela Fishman, Gosia Jaros-White, Joanna Konieczna, Michael Mone, Mary Perrotta Rich, Katarzyna Starzyńska-Kościuszko, Claire Van Poperin, Joseph Vella, Gabby Wu

Text composition: ElectraGraphics, Inc.
Cover Design: EMC Design Ltd
Illustration credits: See Credits page 249.
Photo credits: See Credits page 249.
Audio: CityVox
Development: Blue Crab Editorial Services

Library of Congress Cataloging-in-Publication Data
A catalog record for the print edition is available from the Library of Congress.

ISBN-13: 9780137359240 (Student Book with App and MyEnglishLab)
ISBN-10: 0137359241 (Student Book with App and MyEnglishLab)

ISBN-13: 9780137360307 (Student Book with App)
ISBN-10: 0137360304 (Student Book with App)

Printed in the United States of America
15 2024

pearsonenglish.com

CONTENTS

Welcome to *Future: English for Work, Life, and Academic Success*

Future is a six-level, standards-based English language course for adult and young adult students. *Future* provides students with the contextualized academic language, strategies, and critical-thinking skills needed for success in workplace, life, and academic settings. *Future* is aligned with the requirements of the Workforce Innovation and Opportunity Act (WIOA), the English Language Proficiency (ELP) and College and Career Readiness (CCR) standards, and the National Reporting System (NRS) level descriptors. The 21st century curriculum in *Future*'s second edition helps students acquire the basic literacy, language, and employability skills needed to meet the requirements set by the standards.

Future develops students' academic and critical thinking skills, digital literacy and numeracy, and workplace and civic skills, and it prepares students for taking standardized tests. Competency and skills incorporating standards are in the curriculum at every level, providing a foundation for academic rigor, research-based teaching strategies, corpus-informed language, and the best of digital tools.

In revising the course, we listened to hundreds of *Future* teachers and learners and studied the standards for guidance. *Future* continues to be the most comprehensive English communication course for adults, with its signature scaffolded lessons and multiple practice activities throughout. *Future*'s second edition provides enhanced content, rigorous academic language practice, and cooperative learning through individual and collaborative practice. Every lesson teaches the interpretive, interactive, and productive skills highlighted in the standards.

Future's Instructional Design

Learner Centered and Outcome Oriented

The student is at the center of *Future*. Lessons start by connecting to student experience and knowledge, and then present targeted skills in meaningful contexts. Varied and dynamic skill practice progresses from controlled to independent in a meticulously scaffolded sequence.

Headers highlighting Depth of Knowledge (DOK) terms are used throughout levels 1–4 of *Future* to illuminate the skills being practiced. Every lesson culminates in an activity in which students apply their learning, demonstrate their knowledge, and express themselves orally or in writing. A DOK glossary for teachers includes specific suggestions on how to help students activate these cognitive skills.

Varied Practice

Cognitive science has proven what *Future* always knew: Students learn new skills through varied practice over time. Content-rich units that contextualize academic and employability skills naturally recycle concepts, language, and targeted skills. Individual and collaborative practice activities engage learners and lead to lasting outcomes. Lessons support both student collaboration and individual self-mastery. Students develop the interpretative, productive, and interactive skills identified in the NRS guidelines, while using the four language skills of reading, writing, listening, and speaking.

Goal Setting and Learning Assessment

For optimal learning to take place, students need to be involved in setting goals and in monitoring their own progress. *Future* addresses goal setting in numerous ways. In the Student Book, Unit Goals are identified on the unit opener page. Checkboxes at the end of lessons invite students to evaluate their mastery of the material, and suggest additional online practice.

High-quality assessment aligned to the standards checks student progress and helps students prepare to take standardized tests. The course-based assessment program is available in print and digital formats and includes a bank of customizable test items. Digital tests are assigned by the teacher and reported back in the LMS online gradebook. All levels include a midterm and final test. Test items are aligned with unit learning objectives and standards. The course Placement Test is available in print and digital formats. Test-prep materials are also provided for specific standardized tests.

One Integrated Program

Future provides everything adult English language learners need in one integrated program using the latest digital tools and time-tested print resources.

Integrated Skills Contextualized with Rich Content

Future contextualizes grammar, listening, speaking, pronunciation, reading, writing, and vocabulary in meaningful activities that simulate real workplace, educational, and community settings. A special lesson at the end of each unit highlights soft skills at work. While providing relevant content, *Future* helps build learner knowledge and equips adults for their many roles.

Meeting Work, Life, and Education Goals

Future recognizes that every adult learner brings a unique set of work, life, and academic experiences, as well as a distinct skill set. With its diverse array of print and digital resources, *Future* provides learners with multiple opportunities to practice with contextualized materials to build skill mastery. Specialized lessons for academic and workplace skill development are part of *Future*'s broad array of print and digital resources.

Every unit of *Future*'s *Intro* level contains a Life Skills lesson as well as an English at Work lesson.

Life Skills Lessons

In the second edition, the Life Skills lessons in *Future Intro* continue to provide outstanding coverage of life-skills competencies, basing language teaching on real-life situations that students are likely to encounter and focusing on developing the language and civic-literacy skills required today. In addition, every lesson includes practice with digital skills on a mobile device.

English at Work Lessons

Future Intro has further enhanced its development of workplace skills by adding an English at Work lesson to each unit. This new lesson aims to equip students with the critical interpersonal communication skills needed to succeed in any workplace. Students begin each lesson by completing a model conversation with key words and phrases. Then they work collaboratively to practice similar conversations with new information.

Academic Rigor

Rigor and respect for the ability and experiences of the adult learner have always been central to *Future*. The standards provide the foundation for academic rigor. The reading, writing, listening, and speaking practice requires learners to analyze, use context clues, interpret, cite evidence, build knowledge, support a claim, and summarize from a variety of text formats. Regular practice with complex and content-rich materials develops academic language and builds knowledge. Interactive activities allow for collaboration and exchange of ideas in workplace and academic contexts. *Future* emphasizes rigor by highlighting the critical thinking and problem-solving skills required in each activity.

Reading and Writing

All reading lessons have engaging stories with cross-cultural topics that are interesting and relevant to students' lives. The information-rich texts are further supported by beautiful illustrations that present stories in graphic novel format.

To further strengthen its academic rigor, *Future Intro* has also increased its focus on writing in Show What You Know! activities. With the focus on integrated skills in mind, reading and writing skills are practiced throughout each unit along with the other skills in a highly contextualized way.

Future Grows with Your Student

Future takes learners from absolute beginner level through low-advanced English proficiency, addressing students' abilities and learning priorities at each level. As the levels progress, the curricular content and unit structure change accordingly, with the upper levels incorporating more advanced academic language and skills in the text and in the readings.

Future Intro	Future Level 1	Future Level 2	Future Level 3	Future Level 4	Future Advanced
NRS Beginning ESL Literacy	NRS Low Beginning ESL	NRS High Beginning ESL	NRS Low Intermediate ESL	NRS High Intermediate ESL	NRS Advanced ESL
ELPS Level 1	**ELPS** Level 1	**ELPS** Level 2	**ELPS** Level 3	**ELPS** Level 4	**ELPS** Level 5
CCRS Level A	**CCRS** Level A	**CCRS** Level A	**CCRS** Level B	**CCRS** Level C	**CCRS** Level D
CASAS 180 and below	**CASAS** 181–190	**CASAS** 191–200	**CASAS** 201–210	**CASAS** 211–220	**CASAS** 221–235

The **Pearson Practice English App** provides easy mobile access to all of the audio files, plus Grammar Coach videos and activities, and the new Pronunciation Coach videos. Listen and study on the go—anywhere, any time!

Abundant Opportunities for Student Practice

Student

Student's Book is a complete student resource, including lessons in grammar, listening and speaking, pronunciation, reading, writing, vocabulary, and English at Work, taught and practiced in contextual and interactive activities in the cut eBook.

Online Practice allows online independent self-study and interactive practice in pronunciation, grammar, vocabulary, reading, writing, and listening. The portal includes the popular Grammar Coach videos and new Pronunciation Coach videos and activities.

Workbook—with audio—provides additional practice for each lesson in the Student Book, with new readings and practice in writing, grammar, listening, and speaking, plus activities for new English at Work lessons.

The **Teacher's Edition** includes culture notes, teaching tips, and numerous optional and extension activities, with lesson-by-lesson correlations to CCR and ELP standards. Rubrics are provided for evaluation of students' written and oral communication.

Outstanding Teacher Resources

Teacher

Presentation tool for front-of-classroom projection of the Student Book, includes audio at point of use and pop-up activities, including grammar examples, academic conversation stems, and reader's anticipation guide.

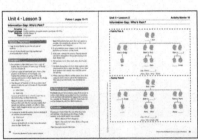

Multilevel Communicative Activities provide an array of reproducible communication activities and games that engage students through different modalities. Teachers' notes provide multilevel options for pre-level and above-level students, as well as extension activities for additional speaking and writing practice.

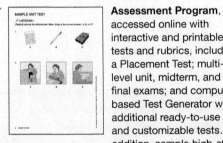

Assessment Program, accessed online with interactive and printable tests and rubrics, includes a Placement Test; multi-level unit, midterm, and final exams; and computer-based Test Generator with additional ready-to-use and customizable tests. In addition, sample high-stakes test practice is included with CASAS test prep for listening and reading.

Go to the Teacher's Portal for easy reference, correlations to federal and state standards, and course updates. pearsonenglish.com

Preview questions activate student background knowledge and help the teacher assess how much students know about the unit theme.

4 Family and Home

PREVIEW

Look at the picture. Who do you see? Why are they together?

A full-page photo introduces the **unit theme** and provides opportunities for interactive classroom discussion.

UNIT GOALS

☐ Identify family members
☐ Say who is in your family
☐ Talk about chores at home
☐ Say months of the year
☐ Write dates

☐ Read and write about home and work
☐ **Life skills:** Fill out a form
☐ **English at work:** Ask about someone's family

65

Unit goals introduce the competencies taught in the unit and allow students to track and reflect on their progress.

UNIT TOUR

Key **vocabulary** is contextualized and practiced in connection to the unit theme.

Model **conversations** present the core competency and language of the lesson.

Lesson 1

That's my brother.

1 VOCABULARY: Family members

A Look at the pictures. What do you see?

▶ Listen and point. Listen and repeat.

B ▶ Listen and read. Listen and repeat.

1. sister	2. brother	3. husband	4. wife
5. grandmother	6. grandfather	7. parents	8. father
9. mother	10. daughter	11. son	12. children

Identify Family Members

2 CONVERSATION

A ▶ Listen. Listen and repeat.

A: Who's that?
B: That's my brother.
A: What's his name?
B: Sam.
A: Who's that?
B: That's my sister.
A: What's her name?
B: Her name is Tina.

B Practice the conversation.

Show what you know!

1. **TALK ABOUT IT.** Show pictures of your family. Ask and answer.

A: Who's that?
B: That's my _____.
A: What's _____ name?
B: _____ name is _____.

2. **WRITE ABOUT IT.** Write the names of your family members.

My sister is Emma.
My mother is Angela.

I can identify family members. ■	I need more practice. ■

Students practice the **conversation** utilizing new **vocabulary** learned in the lesson.

In **Show what you know!**, students apply the target vocabulary in meaningful conversations and in writing.

Grammar is presented in context in model **conversations**.

Grammar charts present the target grammar point in a clear and simple format, providing examples related to the conversation.

Say Who Is in Your Family

Lesson **2** I have two sisters and one brother.

1 CONVERSATION

A ▶ Listen. Listen and repeat.

A: Do you have any sisters or brothers?
B: Yes. I have two sisters and one brother.
A: That's nice. Do you have any children?
B: No, I don't.

B Circle *Yes* or *No*.

1. The woman has two sisters.   Yes   No
2. The woman has two brothers.   Yes   No
3. The woman has children.   Yes   No

C Practice the conversation.

2 READING

A ▶ Listen and read.

Hi, I'm Marta. This is my family. That's my husband. His name is Pedro. My parents are Linda and Roberto. I have two sons, Ernesto and Tino. I have one daughter. Her name is Ana.

Pedro   Marta   Linda   Roberto
Tino   Ernesto   Ana

B Complete the sentences about Marta's family.

1. Pedro is her _____
2. Ana is her _____.
3. Linda is her _____
4. Ernesto and Tino are her _____
5. Roberto and Linda are her _____

Say Who Is in Your Family

3 GRAMMAR: Singular and plural

A ▶ Listen and read. Listen and repeat.

Singular	Plural
one brother	two brothers
a sister	three sisters
one son	two sons
a daughter	three daughters
one parent	two parents
one child	two children

B Match.

__b__ 1. my brother Tom and my brother Mark   **a.** my parents
_____ 2. my son and daughter   **b.** my brothers
_____ 3. my mother and father   **c.** my sisters
_____ 4. my sister Sue and my sister Mary   **d.** my children

Show what you know!

1. TALK ABOUT IT. Ask and answer.

A: *Do you have any sisters or brothers?*
B: _____
A: *Do you have any children?*
B: _____

2. WRITE ABOUT IT. Write sentences.

I have one brother.
I have two daughters.

I can say who is in my family. ■	I need more practice. ■

Target **grammar** is further contextualized in a **reading** passage.

Show what you know! integrates an interactive exchange and a writing task so students demonstrate their mastery of the grammar point using a range of language skills.

UNIT TOUR

Life Skills lessons focus on functional language and practical skills. By introducing real-life materials, such as personal forms, they help students to develop document literacy and civic-literacy skills.

Writing activities incorporate language from the unit. Students then work collaboratively to practice life skills.

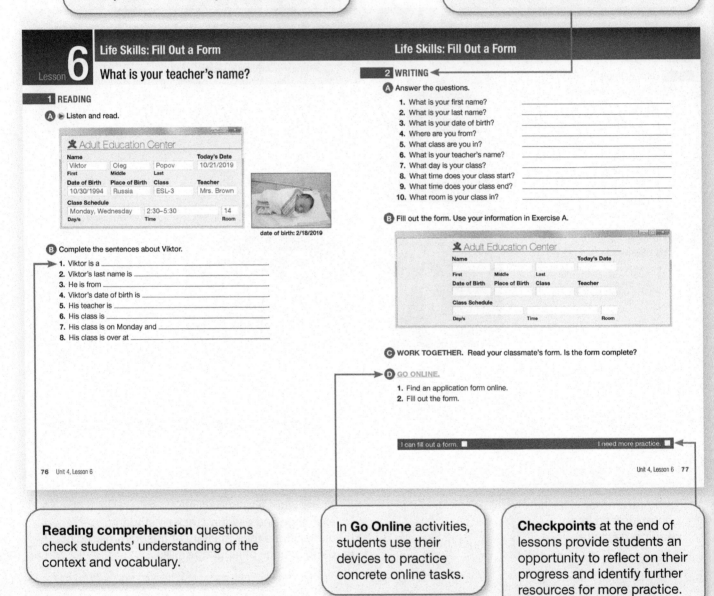

Lesson **6** — Life Skills: Fill Out a Form

What is your teacher's name?

1 READING

A ▶ Listen and read.

Adult Education Center

Name			Today's Date
Viktor	Oleg	Popov	10/21/2019
First	Middle	Last	
Date of Birth	Place of Birth	Class	Teacher
10/30/1994	Russia	ESL-3	Mrs. Brown
Class Schedule			
Monday, Wednesday	2:30–5:30		14
Day/s	Time		Room

date of birth: 2/18/2019

B Complete the sentences about Viktor.

1. Viktor is a _____
2. Viktor's last name is _____
3. He is from _____
4. Viktor's date of birth is _____
5. His teacher is _____
6. His class is _____
7. His class is on Monday and _____
8. His class is over at _____

2 WRITING

A Answer the questions.

1. What is your first name? _____
2. What is your last name? _____
3. What is your date of birth? _____
4. Where are you from? _____
5. What class are you in? _____
6. What is your teacher's name? _____
7. What day is your class? _____
8. What time does your class start? _____
9. What time does your class end? _____
10. What room is your class in? _____

B Fill out the form. Use your information in Exercise A.

Adult Education Center

Name			Today's Date
First	Middle	Last	
Date of Birth	Place of Birth	Class	Teacher
Class Schedule			
Day/s	Time		Room

C WORK TOGETHER. Read your classmate's form. Is the form complete?

D GO ONLINE.

1. Find an application form online.
2. Fill out the form.

I can fill out a form. ☐   I need more practice. ☐

Reading comprehension questions check students' understanding of the context and vocabulary.

In **Go Online** activities, students use their devices to practice concrete online tasks.

Checkpoints at the end of lessons provide students an opportunity to reflect on their progress and identify further resources for more practice.

Lesson 7 — Read and Write About Home and Work

Lucas and Carla are married.

1 LISTENING

A Look at each picture. What do you see?

B ▶ Listen to the story.

Read and Write About Home and Work

2 READING

A ▶ Read and listen.

> Lucas and Carla are married. Lucas is Carla's husband. Carla is Lucas's wife.
> In their native country, men go to work.
> In their native country, women do the household chores.
> In the United States, Carla and Lucas go to work.
> They both do household chores. Lucas washes the dishes.
> Lucas goes to the supermarket, too.

B Circle *Yes* or *No*.

1. Lucas is Carla's husband.   Yes   No
2. In the United States, Carla goes to work.   Yes   No
3. In their native country, women go to work.   Yes   No
4. In the United States, Lucas does household chores.   Yes   No

3 WRITING

A MAKE CONNECTIONS. Talk about work and household chores in your native country.

1. Do men and women go to work?
2. Do women do household chores?
3. Do men do household chores? What household chores do they do?

B Complete the sentences.

1. In my native country, _____ work.
2. _____ do household chores.
3. In the United States, _____ work.
4. _____ do household chores.

C WORK TOGETHER. Read your sentences.

I can read and write about home and work. ☐   I need more practice. ☐

New **English at Work** lessons engage students in real-life situations that develop the personal, social, and cultural skills critical for career success, and help students meet the WIOA requirements.

Lesson **8**

English at Work: Ask About Someone's Family

Mara is at work.

Mara

Co-worker

1 READING

Mara is an assistant.
She works in an office.
She asks her co-worker about her family.

A brief scenario introduces the **character** and the **context** of the conversation.

2 CONVERSATION AT WORK

Ⓐ Complete the conversation. Write the correct words.

Mara:	Is that your family?		
Co-worker:	Yes, it is. That's my _____ and three sisters.	brother	sister
Mara:	_____?	That's nice	Who's that
Co-worker:	That's my _____.	grandmother	grandparents
Mara:	You have a nice family.		
Co-worker:	_____!	You're welcome	Thank you

Ⓑ Practice the conversation.

Ⓒ Role-play the conversation with new information.

I can ask about someone's family. ■	I need more practice. ■

For more practice, go to MyEnglishLab.

80   Unit 4, Lesson 8

Conversation activities are highly scaffolded and progress from controlled to open practice. Students first complete the conversation with key words and phrases. They then proceed to create similar conversations with new information.

Review lessons at the end of each unit provide extra practice for **vocabulary**, **grammar**, **conversation**, **life skills**, and **writing**.

Vocabulary Review includes listening and repeating, categorizing, labeling, and matching exercises.

Grammar Review includes completing charts, writing sentences, and completing conversations.

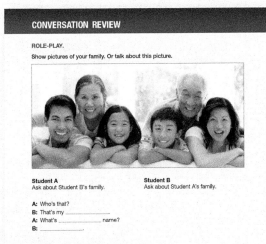

Conversation Review first presents a picture or an illustration that sets the context of the conversation, prompting students' role-play activity that is scaffolded with sentence stems.

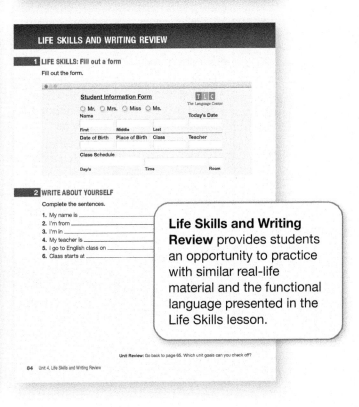

Life Skills and Writing Review provides students an opportunity to practice with similar real-life material and the functional language presented in the Life Skills lesson.

SCOPE AND SEQUENCE

Unit	Vocabulary	Listening and Speaking	Reading	Grammar
Pre-Unit **Getting Started** *page 2*	• Activities in the classroom • The alphabet • Numbers 1–10	• Follow classroom instructions • Understand the alphabet • Understand the numbers	• Locate sections in the book	• Introduction to imperatives
1 **Nice to Meet You** *page 5*	• Countries • The alphabet • Numbers 0–9 • *He, she* • *You, we, they*	• Introduce yourself • Spell first and last names • Say important numbers • Talk about yourself • Introduce someone • Talk about people	• Read a form • Read about greetings	• *I am, you are* • *He is, she is* • *You are, we are, they are*
2 **Welcome to Class** *page 27*	• Classroom items • Classroom instructions • Places in a school • *Next to* • *Across from* • Titles • Study skills	• Ask for things in class • Follow classroom instructions • Talk about places in a school • Describe locations • Talk about study skills	• Read an online form • Read about classrooms	• Imperatives • Simple present: *I, you, we, they*
3 **On Time** *page 47*	• Numbers and time • Daily activities • Days of the week	• Say the time • Talk about time and schedules • Talk about daily activities • Talk about your weekly schedule	• Read a weekly schedule • Read about time	• *From / to, at, on*
4 **Family and Home** *page 65*	• Family members • Household chores • Months and seasons • Dates	• Identify family members • Say who is in your family • Talk about chores at home • Say months of the year • Talk about dates	• Read about someone's family members • Read an application form • Read about home and work	• Singular and plural • *Yes / No* questions

Writing	Document Literacy Numeracy	Life Skills	English At Work
• Write the alphabet • Write the numbers	• Understand numbers 1–10	• Introduce yourself • Understand course numbers and room numbers for school	
• Write first and last names • Write important numbers • Fill out a form • Write about greetings	• Interpret a world map • Read a student ID • Understand an online form	• Read and fill out a form **Digital skill:** • Go online and find your school's website.	• Say hello
• Fill out an online form • Write about classrooms	• Interpret a floor map • Understand an online form	• Understand a form **Digital skill:** • Find a form online and write your information.	• Help someone fill out a form
• Write a weekly schedule • Write about time	• Tell time from a digital clock • Tell time from an analog clock • Interpret daily and weekly schedules	• Read and write a weekly schedule **Digital skill:** • Go online and find the class schedule for your school.	• Talk about schedules
• Write about home and work	• Interpret a yearly calendar • Understand the format of dates	• Fill out a form **Digital skill:** • Find an application form online and fill out the form.	• Ask about someone's family

Text in purple refers to workplace and employability topics.

SCOPE AND SEQUENCE

Unit	Vocabulary	Listening and Speaking	Reading	Grammar
5 **How Much Is It?** *page 85*	• U.S. coins • U.S. bills • Drugstore items • Prices	• Make change with U.S. coins • Make change with U.S. bills • Ask for and say prices	• Read a receipt • Read about shopping	• *Where is, where are*
6 **Let's Eat** *page 103*	• Vegetables • Fruit • Amounts • Containers • Food on a menu	• Talk about vegetables • Say what you like and don't like • Say what someone likes and doesn't like • Ask what someone needs • Order food at a restaurant	• Read an ad • Read a menu • Read about eating	• *Like, don't like* • *Likes, doesn't like*
7 **Apartment for Rent** *page 123*	• Rooms in a home • Words to describe rooms • Furniture and appliances • Addresses	• Identify rooms in a home • Talk about a home • Ask about furniture and appliances • Give an address	• Read an envelope • Read about moving	• *There is, there are* • *Is there, are there*
8 **Let's Go Shopping** *page 141*	• Clothing • Clothing sizes • Colors • Problems with clothing	• Identify clothing you need • Ask for clothing sizes • Describe clothing • Return clothing to a store	• Read a store ad • Read about clothing at a wedding	• *This, that, these, those* • Adjective + noun

Writing	Document Literacy Numeracy	Life Skills	English At Work
• Write about shopping	• Recognize U.S. currency • Understand price tags • Calculate prices • Understand a receipt	• Read a receipt **Digital skill:** • Find an online drugstore and add up the total price of several items you want to buy.	• Answer a customer's questions
• Write shopping lists • Write about eating	• Understand a supermarket ad • Understand a menu • Understand units of measurement	• Read an ad • Make a shopping list **Digital skill:** • Find your favorite supermarket online and write the names and prices of the foods you need to buy.	• Do an inventory
• Write about moving	• Interpret a floor map • Understand apartment ads • Understand an envelope	• Address an envelope • Read an ad **Digital skill:** • Find a business's address online and address an envelope to the business.	• Talk about apartments
• Write about clothing at a wedding	• Interpret store ads	• Read store ads **Digital skill:** • Find a sale on a clothing store website and write the information.	• Help a customer return clothes

Text in purple refers to workplace and employability topics.

SCOPE AND SEQUENCE

Unit	Vocabulary	Listening and Speaking	Reading	Grammar
9 **Our Busy Lives** *page 159*	• Free-time activities • Activities at home • Workplace activities	• Talk about what you do for fun • Talk about what you are doing • Ask about ongoing activities • Talk about ongoing activities at work	• Read the transcript of a voicemail • Read about weekend schedules	• Present continuous • Present continuous: *Yes / No* questions and answers • Present continuous negative
10 **Where's the Bus Stop?** *page 177*	• Places in the community • Public places • Getting to work • Directions • Traffic signs	• Ask about places in the community • Ask where places are • Ask about transportation • Ask for and give directions	• Read about transportation	• *Between, across from*
11 **Get Well Soon** *page 195*	• The body • Medical instructions • Health problems • Emergencies	• Make an appointment • Listen to a doctor • Offer suggestions • Call 911 for emergencies	• Read a medicine label • Read about a doctor's appointment	• *Should*
12 **What Do You Do?** *page 213*	• Jobs • More jobs • Job skills	• Say your occupation • Ask about someone's job • Talk about job skills • Apply for a job	• Read about a job interview	• *Where do / Where does* • *Can*

Writing	Document Literacy Numeracy	Life Skills	English At Work
• Write about weekend schedules	• Interpret a monthly schedule	• Leave a voicemail • Talk about your schedule **Digital skill:** • Use your phone to call a classmate or your teacher and leave a voicemail message.	• Take a personal call
• Write about transportation	• Interpret a street map • Recognize traffic signs	• Read traffic signs **Digital skill:** • Find more traffic signs online and draw one new sign.	• Give directions
• Write about a doctor's appointment	• Understand a medicine label	• Read a medicine label **Digital skill:** • Search online for images of medicine labels and write the instructions.	• Help someone make an appointment
• Write about a job interview	• Read online job ads	• Read a job ad • Fill out a job application **Digital skill:** • Find a job ad online and write the skills you need for the job.	• Apply for a new job

Text in purple refers to workplace and employability topics.

CORRELATIONS

Unit	CASAS Reading Standards (correlated to CASAS Reading Standards 2016)	CASAS Listening Standards (correlated to CASAS Listening Basic Skills Content Standards)
1	**L1:** RDG 1.7, 3.4; **L2:** RDG 1.2, 1.7, 1.8; **L3:** RDG 1.4, 1.7, 1.8; **L4:** RDG 1.7, 1.8, 2.10, 3.4; **L5:** RDG 1.7, 2.9, 2.10; **L6:** RDG 1.7, 2.9, 2.10; **L7:** RDG 1.4, 1.7, 1.8, 3.3; **L8:** RDG 1.7, 1.8, 3.2; **L9:** RDG 1.7, 1.8, 3.2	**L1:** 2.1, 2.3, 4.1, 4.2; **L2:** 2.1, 2.2, 4.1, 4.2; **L3:** 2.1, 4.1, 4.2; **L4:** 2.1, 2.3, 3.3, 4.1, 4.2; **L5:** 2.1, 2.3, 3.1, 3.3, 4.1, 4.2; **L6:** 2.1, 2.3, 3.1, 3.2, 3.3, 4.1, 4.2; **L7:** 2.1, 2.3, 4.2; **L8:** 2.1, 2.3, 4.1, 4.2; **L9:** 2.1, 2.3
2	**L1:** RDG 1.7, 1.8, 2.3; **L2:** RDG 1.7, 1.8, 2.10; **L3:** RDG 1.7, 1.8, 2.3; **L4:** RDG 1.7, 1.8, 3.4; **L5:** RDG 1.4, 1.7, 1.8, 3.3; **L6:** RDG 1.7, 2.9, 2.10; **L7:** RDG 1.8, 3.2; **L8:** RDG 1.7, 1.8, 3.2	**L1:** 2.1, 2.3, 4.1, 4.2; **L2:** 3.4, 4.1, 4.2, 5.4; **L3:** 2.1, 2.3, 4.1, 4.2; **L4:** 2.1, 2.3, 4.1, 4.2; **L5:** 2.1, 4.2; **L6:** 2.1, 2.3, 2.4, 3.1, 3.2, 4.1, 4.2; **L7:** 2.1, 2.4, 4.2; **L8:** 2.1, 2.3, 2.4, 4.1, 4.2
3	**L1:** RDG 1.4; **L2:** RDG 1.4, 1.7, 1.8, 2.9, 2.10; **L3:** RDG 1.4, 1.7, 1.8; **L4:** RDG 1.7, 1.8, 3.2; **L5:** RDG 1.4, 1.7, 1.8, 3.2; **L6:** RDG 1.4, 1.7, 1.8, 3.2; **L7:** RDG 1.4, 1.7, 1.8, 3.2	**L1:** 2.1, 4.2; **L2:** 2.1, 2.3, 4.2; **L3:** 2.1, 2.3, 2.4, 4.1, 4.2; **L4:** 2.4, 3.1, 4.2; **L6:** 2.1, 2.3, 4.1, 4.2; **L7:** 2.1, 2.3, 4.1, 4.2
4	**L1:** RDG 1.7, 1.8; **L2:** RDG 1.7, 1.8, 2.10; **L3:** RDG 1.7, 1.8, 2.3, 2.9, 2.10; **L4:** RDG 1.4, 1.7, 1.8, 2.1; **L5:** RDG 1.4, 1.7, 1.8; **L6:** RDG 1.7, 3.3; **L7:** RDG 1.8, 3.2; **L8:** RDG 1.7, 1.8, 3.2	**L1:** 2.1, 2.3, 4.1, 4.2; **L2:** 3.7, 4.1, 4.2; **L3:** 2.1, 2.3, 3.6, 4.1, 4.2; **L4:** 2.1, 2.3, 4.1, 4.2, 4.3; **L5:** 2.1, 2.3, 4.1, 4.2; **L6:** 2.1, 2.3, 4.2; **L7:** 2.1, 2.4, 4.2; **L8:** 2.1, 2.3, 4.1, 4.2
5	**L1:** RDG 1.4, 1.7, 1.8; **L2:** RDG 1.4, 1.7, 1.8; **L3:** RDG 1.7, 1.8; **L4:** RDG 1.4, 1.7, 1.8; **L5:** RDG 1.4, 1.7, 1.8; **L6:** RDG 1.7, 3.2; **L7:** RDG 1.4, 1.7, 1.8, 3.2	**L1:** 2.1, 2.3, 4.1, 4.2; **L2:** 2.1, 2.3, 4.1, 4.2; **L3:** 2.1, 2.3, 3.6, 4.1, 4.2; **L4:** 2.1, 2.3, 3.6, 4.1, 4.2; **L5:** 2.1, 2.3, 4.1, 4.2; **L6:** 2.1, 2.3, 4.2; **L7:** 2.1, 2.3, 4.1, 4.2
6	**L1:** RDG 1.7, 1.8; **L2:** RDG 1.7, 1.8, 2.10; **L3:** RDG 1.7, 1.8, 2.10, 3.2; **L4:** RDG 1.4, 1.7, 1.8; **L5:** RDG 1.4, 1.7, 1.8, 2.1, 2.2; **L6:** RDG 1.4, 1.7; **L7:** RDG 1.8, 3.2; **L8:** RDG 1.7, 1.8, 3.2	**L1:** 2.1, 2.3, 4.1, 4.2; **L2:** 3.3, 4.1, 4.2, 4.3; **L3:** 3.3, 4.1, 4.2, 4.3; **L4:** 2.1, 2.3, 3.7, 4.1, 4.2, 4.3; **L5:** 2.1, 2.3, 2.4, 4.1, 4.2; **L6:** 2.1, 2.3, 2.4, 4.2; **L7:** 2.1, 2.4, 4.2; **L8:** 2.1, 2.3, 4.1, 4.2, 4.3
7	**L1:** RDG 1.7, 1.8, 3.4; **L2:** RDG 1.7, 1.8, 3.4; **L3:** RDG 1.7, 1.8, 2.10, 3.4; **L4:** RDG 1.4, 1.7, 1.8; **L5:** RDG 1.4, 1.7, 1.8, 2.2; **L6:** RDG 1.7, 3.2; **L7:** RDG 1.7, 1.8, 3.2	**L1:** 2.1, 2.3, 4.1, 4.2; **L2:** 2.1, 2.3, 3.1, 4.1, 4.2; **L3:** 2.1, 2.3, 3.1, 3.3, 4.1, 4.2; **L4:** 2.1, 2.3, 4.1, 4.2; **L6:** 2.1, 2.3, 4.2; **L7:** 2.1, 2.3, 4.1, 4.2
8	**L1:** RDG 1.7, 1.8; **L2:** RDG 1.7, 1.8, 2.9, 2.10; **L3:** RDG 1.7, 1.8, 2.9, 2.10; **L4:** RDG 1.7, 1.8; **L5:** RDG 1.4, 1.7, 1.8, 2.2; **L6:** RDG 1.7, 3.2; **L7:** RDG 1.7, 1.8, 3.2	**L1:** 2.1, 2.3, 4.1, 4.2; **L2:** 2.1, 2.3, 4.1, 4.2; **L3:** 2.1, 2.3, 4.1, 4.2; **L4:** 2.1, 2.3, 4.1, 4.2; **L6:** 2.1, 2.3, 4.1, 4.2; **L7:** 2.1, 2.3, 4.1, 4.2
9	**L1:** RDG 1.4, 1.7, 1.8, 3.4; **L2:** RDG 1.7, 1.8, 2.9, 2.10, 3.2; **L3:** RDG 1.7, 1.8, 2.9, 2.10; **L4:** RDG 1.7, 1.8, 2.9, 2.10; **L5:** RDG 1.7, 1.8; **L6:** RDG 1.7, 3.2; **L7:** RDG 1.7, 1.8, 3.2	**L1:** 2.1, 2.3, 4.1, 4.2; **L2:** 2.1, 2.3, 3.9, 4.1, 4.2; **L3:** 2.1, 2.3, 3.6, 3.9, 4.1, 4.2; **L4:** 2.1, 2.3, 3.9, 4.1, 4.2; **L5:** 2.1, 2.3, 4.2; **L6:** 2.1, 2.3, 4.1, 4.2; **L7:** 2.1, 2.3, 4.1, 4.2
10	**L1:** RDG 1.7, 1.8, 3.4; **L2:** RDG 1.7, 1.8, 3.4; **L3:** RDG 1.7, 1.8; **L4:** RDG 1.7, 1.8, 3.4; **L5:** RDG 1.3, 1.7, 1.8; **L6:** RDG 1.7, 1.8, 3.2; **L7:** RDG 1.7, 1.8, 3.2	**L1:** 2.1, 2.3, 4.1, 4.2; **L2:** 2.1, 2.3, 4.1, 4.2; **L3:** 2.1, 2.3, 4.1, 4.2; **L4:** 2.1, 2.3, 4.1, 4.2; **L5:** 2.1, 2.3, 4.2; **L6:** 2.1, 2.3, 4.1, 4.2; **L7:** 2.1, 2.3, 4.1, 4.2
11	**L1:** RDG 1.4, 1.7, 1.8; **L2:** RDG 1.7, 1.8; **L3:** RDG 1.7, 1.8; **L4:** RDG 1.7, 1.8, 3.4; **L5:** RDG 1.3, 1.4, 1.7, 1.8, 2.2; **L6:** RDG 1.7, 1.8, 3.2; **L7:** RDG 1.7, 1.8, 3.2	**L1:** 2.1, 2.3, 4.1, 4.2; **L2:** 2.1, 2.3, 4.1, 4.2; **L3:** 2.1, 2.3, 4.1, 4.2; **L4:** 2.1, 2.3, 4.1, 4.2; **L5:** 2.1, 2.3, 4.2; **L6:** 2.1, 2.3, 4.1, 4.2; **L7:** 2.1, 2.3, 4.1, 4.2
12	**L1:** RDG 1.7, 1.8; **L2:** RDG 1.7, 1.8, 2.9, 2.10; **L3:** RDG 1.7, 1.8; **L4:** RDG 1.7, 1.8, 2.9, 2.10; **L5:** RDG 1.4, 1.7, 1.8; **L6:** RDG 1.7, 1.8, 3.2; **L7:** RDG 1.7, 1.8, 3.2	**L1:** 2.1, 2.3, 4.1, 4.2; **L2:** 2.1, 2.3, 3.6, 4.1, 4.2; **L3:** 2.1, 2.3, 4.1, 4.2; **L4:** 2.1, 2.3, 3.1, 3.9, 4.1, 4.2; **L5:** 2.1, 2.3, 4.2; **L6:** 2.1, 2.3, 4.1, 4.2; **L7:** 2.1, 2.3, 4.1, 4.2

CASAS: Comprehensive Adult Student Assessment System
CCRS: College and Career Readiness Standards (R=Reading; W=Writing; SL=Speaking/Listening; L=Language)
ELPS: English Language Proficiency Standards

CASAS Competencies (correlated to CASAS Competencies: Essential Life and Work skills for Youth and Adults)	CCRS Correlations, Level A	ELPS Correlations, Level 1
L1: 0.1.2, 0.1.4, 0.1.5, 0.2.1; **L2:** 0.1.2, 0.1.5, 0.2.1; **L3:** 0.1.2, 0.1.5, 0.2.1; **L4:** 0.1.2, 0.1.5, 0.2.1; **L5:** 0.1.2, 0.1.4, 0.1.5; **L6:** 0.1.2, 0.1.4, 0.1.5; **L7:** 0.1.2, 0.1.5, 0.2.2, 2.8.5; 7.4.4, 7.7.3; **L8:** 0.1.1, 0.1.2, 0.1.4, 0.1.5; **L9:** 0.1.2, 0.1.4, 0.1.5	**L1:** SL1.1, SL.K.3, L1.5a, L1.5c, L1.6; **L2:** SL1.1, L1.1a; **L4:** SL1.4, SL.K.6, L1.1c, L1.1d, L1.1e, L1.1g, L1.1I; **L5:** SL1.4, SL.K.6, L1.1c, L1.1d, L1.1e, L1.1g, L1.1I; **L6:** SL.1.4, L1.1c, L.1.1d, L.1.1e, L.1.1g, L.1.1I, L.1.6; **L7:** W.1.7, W.1.8; **L8:** RI/RL.1.1, RI.1.4, RI.1.7, SL.K.2	ELPS 1–3, 5, 7–9
L1: 0.1.2, 0.1.4, 0.1.5, 0.2.1; **L2:** 0.1.5, 0.1.7; **L3:** 0.1.2, 0.1.5; **L4:** 0.1.2, 0.1.5, 2.2.1; **L5:** 0.1.2, 0.1.5, 0.2.2, 2.8.5; 7.4.4, 7.7.3; **L6:** 0.1.2, 0.1.5, 0.2.1, 7.4.1; **L7:** 0.1.2, 0.1.5, 0.2.1, 4.4.3; **L8:** 0.1.2, 0.1.5, 0.2.1	**L1:** SL.1.4, SL.K.6, L.1.5a, L.1.5c, L.1.6; **L2:** SL.K.3, L.1.1I, L.1.6; **L3:** SL.1.1, SL.K.6, L.1.5a, L.1.6; **L4:** SL.1.1, L.1.1j; **L5:** RI/RL.1.1, W.1.7, W.1.8; **L6:** L.1.1e, L.1.1g; **L7:** RI/RL.1.1, RI.1.2, RI.1.3, RI.1.4, RI.1.7, SL.K.2	ELPS 1–3, 5, 7–10
L1: 0.1.2, 0.1.5, 2.3.1; **L2:** 0.1.2, 0.1.5, 2.3.1; **L3:** 0.1.2, 0.1.5, 0.2.1, 2.3.1; **L4:** 0.1.2, 0.1.5, 2.8.3; **L5:** 0.1.2, 0.1.5, 2.8.3, 7.4.4, 7.7.3; **L6:** 0.1.2, 0.1.5; **L7:** 0.1.2, 0.1.4, 0.1.5, 4.6.1	**L1:** SL.1.1, SL.K.3, SL.K.6, L.1.5a, L.1.5c, L.1.6; **L2:** SL.1.4, L.1.1j, L.1.1I, L.1.6; **L3:** SL.1.1, SL.K.3, SL.K.6, L.1.5a, L.1.5c, L.1.6; **L4:** L.1.1j, L.1.2b; **L5:** RI/RL.1.1, RI.1.2, W.1.2, W.1.7, W.1.8, SL.K.2; **L6:** RI/RL.1.1, RI.1.2, RI.1.4, RI.1.7, SL.K.2; **L7:** RI/RL.1.1, RI.1.2, RI.1.3, RI.1.4, RI.1.7, SL.K.2	ELPS 1–3, 5, 7–10
L1: 0.1.2, 0.1.5, 0.2.1; **L2:** 0.1.2, 0.1.5, 0.2.1; **L3:** 0.1.2, 0.1.5; **L4:** 0.1.2, 0.1.5, 0.1.8, 2.3.2; **L5:** 0.1.2, 0.1.4, 0.1.5, 2.3.2; **L6:** 0.1.2, 0.1.5, 0.2.1, 2.8.5, 7.4.4, 7.7.3; **L7:** 0.1.2, 0.1.5, 0.2.1, 7.5.5, 8.2.3; **L8:** 0.1.2, 0.1.4, 0.1.5	**L1:** SL.K.3, SL.K.6, L.1.6; **L2:** SL.1.1, SL.K.3, L.1.1b, L.1.1c; **L3:** SL.1.1, SL.K.2, L.1.1k, L.1.1I, L.1.2c, L.1.2d, L.1.5c, L.1.6; **L4:** L.1.2b, L.1.5a, L.1.6; **L5:** SL.1.4, SL.K.6 RI/RL.1.1, RI.1.2, W.1.2, W.1.7, W.1.8, SL.K.2; **L6:** RI/RL.1.1, RI.1.2, W.1.7, W.1.8; **L7:** RI/RL.1.1, RI.1.2, RI.1.3, RI.1.4, RI.1.7	ELPS 1–3, 5, 7–10
L1: 0.1.2, 0.1.5, 1.1.6; **L2:** 0.1.2, 0.1.5, 1.1.6; **L3:** 0.1.2, 0.1.5, 1.4.1; **L4:** 0.1.2, 0.1.5, 1.1.6, 1.4.1; **L5:** 0.1.2, 0.1.5, 1.1.6, 1.6.4, 7.4.4, 7.7.3; **L6:** 0.1.2, 0.1.5, 1.2.2; **L7:** 0.1.2, 0.1.4, 0.1.5, 1.1.6	**L1:** SL.1.4, L.1.6; **L2:** SL.1.1, SL.K.2, L.1.6; **L3:** SL.K.2, SL.K.3, SL.K.6, L.1.1k, L.1.1I, L.1.5a, L.1.5c, L.1.6; **L4:** SL.K.3, SL.K.6; **L5:** RI/RL.1.1, RI.1.2, W.1.7, W.1.8, L.1.5c; **L6:** RI/RL.1.1, RI.1.2, RI.1.3, RI.1.4, RI.1.7; **L7:** RI/RL.1.1, RI.1.2, RI.1.3, RI.1.4, RI.1.7	ELPS 1–3, 5, 7–10
L1: 0.1.2, 0.1.4, 0.1.5, 0.1.6, 1.2.8; **L2:** 0.1.2, 0.1.5, 0.2.1; **L3:** 0.1.2, 0.1.5, 0.2.1; **L4:** 0.1.2, 0.1.5, 1.1.6, 1.2.8; **L5:** 0.1.2, 0.1.5, 1.1.6, 1.2.8, 7.4.4, 7.7.3; **L6:** 0.1.2, 0.1.5, 1.1.6, 0.2.1, 2.6.4; **L7:** 0.1.2, 0.1.5, 2.7.9; **L8:** 0.1.2, 0.1.5	**L1:** SL.1.1, L.1.5c, L.1.6; **L2:** L.1.1c; **L3:** SL.1.1, SL.K.6, L.1.1c, L.1.1I, L.1.5c, L.1.6; **L4:** SL.K.6, L.1.1c, L.1.5a, L.1.6; **L5:** RI/RL.1.1, RI.1.4, RI.1.7, W.1.7, W.1.8; **L6:** SL.1.4; **L7:** RI/RL.1.1, RI.1.2, RI.1.3, SL.K.2, SL.K.3	ELPS 1–10
L1: 0.1.2, 0.1.5, 1.4.1; **L2:** 0.1.2, 0.1.5, 1.4.1; **L3:** 0.1.2, 0.1.5, 1.4.1; **L4:** 0.1.2, 0.1.5, 1.1.6, 1.4.4, 1.4.2; **L5:** 0.1.2, 0.1.5, 0.2.3, 2.4.1, 7.4.4, 7.7.3; **L6:** 0.1.2, 0.1.4, 0.1.5; **L7:** 0.1.2, 0.1.5, 1.1.6, 1.4.1, 1.4.2	**L1:** SL.1.4, SL.K.6, L.1.6; **L2:** SL.1.1, SL.K.6, L.1.1I, L.1.6; **L3:** SL.1.1, SL.K.3, L.1.1k, L.1.5a, L.1.5c; **L5:** RI/RL.1.1, RI.1.4, W.1.7, W.1.8; **L6:** RI/RL.1.1, RI.1.2, RI.1.3, SL.K.2, SL.K.3; **L7:** RI/RL.1.1, RI.1.2, RI.1.3, RI.1.7, SL.K.2, SL.K.3	ELPS 1–3, 5, 7–10
L1: 0.1.2, 0.1.5, 1.2.9; **L2:** 0.1.2, 0.1.4, 0.1.5, 1.2.9; **L3:** 0.1.2, 0.1.4, 0.1.5, 1.2.9; **L4:** 0.1.2, 0.1.5, 1.2.9, 1.3.3; **L5:** 0.1.2, 0.1.5, 1.2.2, 1.2.9, 7.4.4, 7.7.3; **L6:** 0.1.2, 0.1.5, 1.2.9, 2.7.2, 2.7.9; **L7:** 0.1.2, 0.1.4, 0.1.5, 1.3.3	**L1:** SL.1.1, SL.K.3, L.1.5c, L.1.6; **L2:** SL.1.1, SL.K.6, L.1.6; **L3:** SL.K.3, SL.1.4, SL.K.6, L.1.1b, L.1.1f, L.1.1g, L.1.1I, L.1.5c; **L4:** L.1.6; **L5:** RI/RL.1.1, RI.1.4, RI.1.7, W.1.7, W.1.8, SL.K.2; **L6:** RI/RL.1.1, RI.1.2, RI.1.3, RI.1.7, SL.K.2	ELPS 1–3, 7–10
L1: 0.1.2, 0.1.5, 0.2.4; **L2:** 0.1.2, 0.1.4, 0.1.5, 0.2.4; **L3:** 0.1.2, 0.1.4, 0.1.5, 0.2.4; **L4:** 0.1.2, 0.1.5, 1.2.9, 4.1.6; **L5:** 0.1.2, 0.1.5, 2.1.7, 2.1.8, 4.6.5, 7.4.4, 7.7.3; **L6:** 0.1.2, 0.1.5, 0.2.4; **L7:** 0.1.2, 0.1.4, 0.1.5, 4.6.5, 4.8.1	**L1:** SL.1.1, SL.K.6, L.1.5a, L.1.5c, L.1.6; **L2:** SL.1.1, SL.1.3, L.1.1e, L.1.1g; **L3:** SL.K.3, SL.1.4, SL.K.6, L.1.1e, L.1.1g, L.1.1I, L.1.5c; **L4:** L.1.1I, L.1.5c, L.1.6; **L5:** RI/RL.1.1, W.1.7, W.1.8; **L6:** RI/RL.1.1, RI.1.2, RI.1.3, RI.1.4, RI.1.7, SL.K.2; **L7:** RI/RL.1.1, RI.1.2, RI.1.3, RI.1.7, SL.K.2	ELPS 1–3, 5, 7–10
L1: 0.1.2, 0.1.4, 0.1.5, 2.2.1; **L2:** 0.1.2, 0.1.4, 0.1.5, 2.2.1; **L3:** 0.1.2, 0.1.4, 0.1.5, 2.2.3; **L4:** 0.1.2, 0.1.4, 0.1.5, 2.2.1; **L5:** 0.1.2, 0.1.5, 1.9.1, 7.4.4, 7.7.3; **L6:** 0.1.2, 0.1.4, 0.1.5, 2.2.3; **L7:** 0.1.7, 2.2.1, 4.8.3	**L1:** SL.1.1, L.1.1I, L.1.5c, L.1.6; **L2:** SL.1.1, L.1.1j, L.1.5c, L.1.6; **L3:** SL.K.2, SL.1.4, SL.K.6, L.1.5a, L.1.5c, L.1.6; **L4:** RI.1.7, SL.K.3, SL.K.6; **L5:** W.1.7, W.1.8; **L6:** RI/RL.1.1, RI.1.2, RI.1.3, RI.1.4, RI.1.7, SL.K.2; **L7:** RI/RL.1.1, RI.1.2, RI.1.3, RI.1.7, SL.K.2	ELPS 1–3, 5, 7–10
L1: 0.1.2, 0.1.4, 0.1.5, 3.1.2, 3.6.1; **L2:** 0.1.2, 0.1.4, 0.1.5, 3.6.3, 3.6.4; **L3:** 0.1.2, 0.1.4, 0.1.5, 3.6.3; **L4:** 0.1.2, 0.1.4, 0.1.5, 1.9.7, 2.1.2, 2.2.1, 3.6.3; **L5:** 0.1.2, 0.1.5, 3.3.1, 3.3.2, 7.4.4, 7.7.3; **L6:** 0.1.2, 0.1.5, 2.7.9, 3.1.2; **L7:** 0.1.2, 0.1.4, 0.1.5, 3.1.2. 3.6.3, 3.6.4	**L1:** SL.1.1, L.1.5c, L.1.6; **L2:** SL.1.1, SL.K.6, L.1.5c; **L3:** L.1.1I, L.1.5c; **L4:** SL.1.4, SL.K.6; **L5:** RI/RL.1.1, RI.1.4, W.1.7, W.1.8; **L6:** RI/RL.1.1, RI.1.2, RI.1.3, RI.1.4, RI.1.7, SL.K.2, SL.K.3; **L7:** SL.K.3	ELPS 1–3, 5, 7–10
L1: 0.1.2, 0.1.4, 0.1.5, 4.1.8; **L2:** 0.1.2, 0.1.4, 0.1.5, 4.1.8; **L3:** 0.1.2, 0.1.4, 0.1.5, 4.1.5, 4.1.6, 4.1.8; **L4:** 0.1.2, 0.1.4, 0.1.5, 4.1.2; **L5:** 0.1.2, 0.1.4, 0.1.5, 4.1.3, 7.4.4, 7.7.3; **L6:** 0.1.2, 0.1.5, 4.1.5, 4.1.7; **L7:** 0.1.2, 0.1.4, 0.1.5, 4.1.5, 4.1.7	**L1:** SL.K.2, L.1.5a, L.1.5c, L.1.6; **L2:** SL.1.1, SL.K.2, SL.K.3, SL.1.4, SL.K.6, L.1.1k, L.1.5c, L.1.6; **L3:** SL.1.1, SL.K.6, L.1.5c, L.1.6; **L4:** SL.K.3, L.1.1k, L.1.1I; **L5:** RI/RL.1.1, W.1.7, W.1.8; **L6:** RI.1.2, RI.1.3, RI.1.4, RI.1.7	ELPS 1–3, 5, 7–10

All units of *Future* meet most of the **EFF Content Standards**. For details, as well as for correlations to other state standards, go to www.pearsoneltusa.com/future 2e.

SERIES CONSULTANT AND LEARNING EXPERT

Sarah Lynn is an ESOL teacher trainer, author, and curriculum design specialist. She has taught adult learners in the U.S. and abroad for decades, most recently at Harvard University's Center for Workforce Development. As a teacher-trainer and frequent conference presenter throughout the United States and Latin America, Ms. Lynn has led sessions and workshops on topics such as fostering student agency and resilience, brain-based teaching techniques, literacy and learning, and teaching in a multilevel classroom. Collaborating with program leaders, teachers, and students, she has developed numerous curricula for college and career readiness, reading and writing skill development, and contextualized content for adult English language learners. Ms. Lynn has co-authored several Pearson ELT publications, including *Business Across Cultures, Future, Future U.S. Citizens,* and *Project Success.* She holds a master's degree in TESOL from Teachers College, Columbia University.

SERIES CONSULTANTS

Ronna Magy has worked as an ESOL classroom teacher, author, teacher-trainer, and curriculum development specialist. She served as the ESL Teacher Adviser in charge of professional development for the Division of Adult and Career Education of the Los Angeles Unified School District. She is a frequent conference presenter on the College and Career Readiness Standards (CCRS), the English Language Proficiency Standards (ELPS), and on the language, literacy, and soft skills needed for academic and workplace success. Ms. Magy has authored/ co-authored and trained teachers on modules for CALPRO, the California Adult Literacy Professional Development Project, including modules on integrating and contextualizing workforce skills in the ESOL classroom and evidence-based writing instruction. She is the author of adult ESL publications on English for the workplace, reading and writing, citizenship, and life skills and test preparation. Ms. Magy holds a master's degree in social welfare from the University of California at Berkeley.

Federico Salas-Isnardi has worked in adult education as a teacher, administrator, professional developer, materials writer, and consultant. He contributed to a number of state projects in Texas including the adoption of adult education content standards and the design of statewide professional development and accountability systems.

Over nearly 30 years he has conducted professional development seminars for thousands of teachers, law enforcement officers, social workers, and business people in the United States and abroad. His areas of concentration have been educational leadership, communicative competence, literacy, intercultural communication, citizenship, and diversity education. He has taught customized workplace ESOL and Spanish programs as well as high-school equivalence classes, citizenship and civics, labor market information seminars, and middle-school mathematics. Mr. Salas-Isnardi has been a contributing writer or series consultant for a number of ESL publications, and he has co-authored curriculum for site-based workforce ESL and Spanish classes.

Mr. Salas-Isnardi is a certified diversity trainer. He has a master's degree in Applied Linguistics and doctoral level coursework in adult education.

AUTHOR

Yvonne Wong Nishio has been an adult school teacher, curriculum coordinator, counselor, and resource/demonstration teacher over the past 37 years in the Los Angeles Unified School District (LAUSD). She has taught all six ESL levels at Evans Community Adult School, one of the largest adult learning centers in the country. Ms. Nishio developed curriculum as well as materials for the Division of Adult and Career Education of LAUSD, including the *Asian Project,* which pioneered ESL materials culturally relevant to Asian Pacific immigrants; *Holidays in the U.S.,* which highlighted the multicultural roots of American holidays and customs; and *Places to See in the Los Angeles Area.* Ms. Nishio prepared a video program on domestic violence, *To Ensure Domestic Tranquility,* through a grant from the American Bar Association. Ms. Nishio's extensive work in ESL literacy includes contributions to the ESL Language Model Standards for Adult Education Programs established by the California Department of Education as well as the successful books *Longman ESL Literacy,* now in its third edition, and Longman *ESL Literacy Teacher's Resource Book.*

ACKNOWLEDGMENTS

The Publisher would like to acknowledge the teachers, students, and survey and focus-group participants for their valuable input. Thank you to the following reviewers and consultants who made suggestions, contributed to this *Future* revision, and helped make *Future: English for Work, Life, and Academic Success* even better in this second edition. There are many more who also shared their comments and experiences using *Future*—a big thank you to all.

Fuad Al-Daraweesh The University of Toledo, Toledo, OH

Denise Alexander Bucks County Community College, Newtown, PA

Isabel Alonso Bergen Community College, Hackensack, NJ

Veronica Avitia LeBarron Park, El Paso, TX

Maria Bazan-Myrick Houston Community College, Houston, TX

Sara M. Bulnes Miami Dade College, Miami, FL

Alexander Chakshiri Santa Maria High School, Santa Maria, CA

Scott C. Cohen, M.A.Ed. Bergen Community College, Paramus, NJ

Judit Criado Fiuza Mercy Center, Bronx, NY

Megan Ernst Glendale Community College, Glendale, CA

Rebecca Feit-Klein Essex County College Adult Learning Center, West Caldwell, NJ

Caitlin Floyd Nationalities Service Center, Philadelphia, PA

Becky Gould International Community High School, Bronx, NY

Ingrid Greenberg San Diego Continuing Education, San Diego Community College District, San Diego, CA

Steve Gwynne San Diego Continuing Education, San Diego, CA

Robin Hatfield, M.Ed. Learning Institute of Texas, Houston,TX

Coral Horton Miami Dade College, Kendall Campus, Miami, FL

Roxana Hurtado Miami-Dade County Public Schools, Miami, FL

Lisa Johnson City College of San Francisco, San Francisco, CA

Kristine R. Kelly ATLAS @ Hamline University, St. Paul, MN

Jennifer King Austin Community College, Austin, TX

Lia Lerner, Ed.D. Burbank Adult School, Burbank, CA

Ting Li The University of Toledo, Ottawa Hills, OH

Nichole M. Lucas University of Dayton, Dayton, OH

Ruth Luman Modesto Junior College, Modesto, CA

Josephine Majul El Monte-Rosemead Adult School, El Monte, CA

Dr. June Ohrnberger Suffolk County Community College, Selden, NY

Sue Park The Learning Institute of Texas, Houston, TX

Dr. Sergei Paromchik Adult Education Department, Hillsborough County Public Schools, Tampa, FL

Patricia Patton Uniontown ESL, Uniontown, PA

Matthew Piech Amarillo College, Amarillo, TX

Guillermo Rocha Essex County College, NJ

Audrene Rowe Essex County School, Newark, NJ

Naomi Sato Glendale Community College, Glendale, CA

Alejandra Solis Lone Star College, Houston, TX

Geneva Tesh Houston Community College, Houston, TX

Karyna Tytar Lake Washington Institute of Technology, Kirkland, WA

Miguel Veloso Miami Springs Adult, Miami, FL

Minah Woo Howard Community College, Columbia, MD

1 MEET YOUR TEACHER

Look at the teacher and student.
▶ Listen and point. Listen and repeat.

2 CLASSROOM INSTRUCTIONS

A Look at the actions.
▶ Listen and point. Listen and repeat.

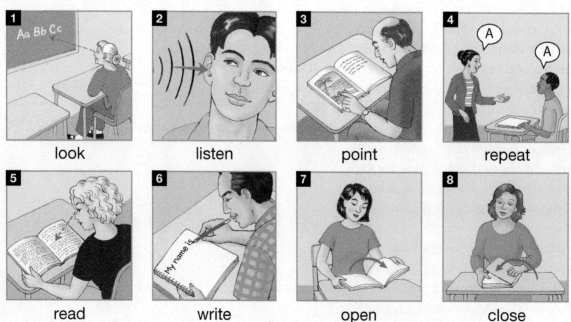

look	listen	point	repeat
read	write	open	close

B **WORK TOGETHER.** Point to a picture in Exercise A. Say the action.

3 ASK FOR HELP

Look at the pictures. Complete the conversations.

~~Can you speak more slowly?~~   Can you repeat that?

What does this word mean?   What's this called in English?

1.

- Where are you from?
- I'm sorry. *Can you speak more slowly?*
- Oh, sorry. Where are you from?
- I'm from Korea.

2.

- _____
- It's a pencil sharpener.
- Thank you.

3.

- Can you help me?
- Sure.
- _____
- Occupation? It means a job or career.

4.

- Please turn to page 45.
- Sure. Please turn to page 45.
- I'm sorry. _____ _____

4 SAY THE ALPHABET

Look at the alphabet.
▶ Listen and read. Listen and repeat.

Aa Bb Cc Dd Ee

Ff Gg Hh Ii Jj Kk

Ll Mm Nn Oo Pp

Qq Rr Ss Tt Uu

Vv Ww Xx Yy Zz

5 SAY NUMBERS

Look at the numbers.
▶ **Listen and point. Listen and repeat.**

| 1 | 2 | 3 | 4 | 5 | 6 | 7 | 8 | 9 | 10 |

6 LEARN ABOUT *FUTURE*

Ⓐ Turn to page iii. Answer the questions.

1. How many units are in this book? _____
2. Which unit is about families? _____
3. Which unit is about health? _____
4. Which unit is about food? _____
5. Which unit is about shopping? _____
6. Which unit is about school? _____

Ⓑ Look in the back of your book. Find each section. Write the page numbers.

Map of the World _____

Word List _____

Audio Script _____

Index _____

Map of the United States and Canada _____

Ⓒ Look inside the front cover. How will you get the Pearson Practice English app with audio?

_____

1 Nice to Meet You

PREVIEW

Look at the picture. Who do you see?
What are they doing?

UNIT GOALS

- ☐ Introduce yourself
- ☐ Spell first and last names
- ☐ Say and write important numbers
- ☐ Talk about yourself
- ☐ Introduce someone

- ☐ Talk about people
- ☐ Read and write about greetings
- ☐ **Life skills:** Read and fill out a form
- ☐ **English at work:** Say hello

Lesson 1 Where are you from?

1 VOCABULARY: Countries

A Look at the map. What do you see?

▶ Listen and point. Listen and repeat.

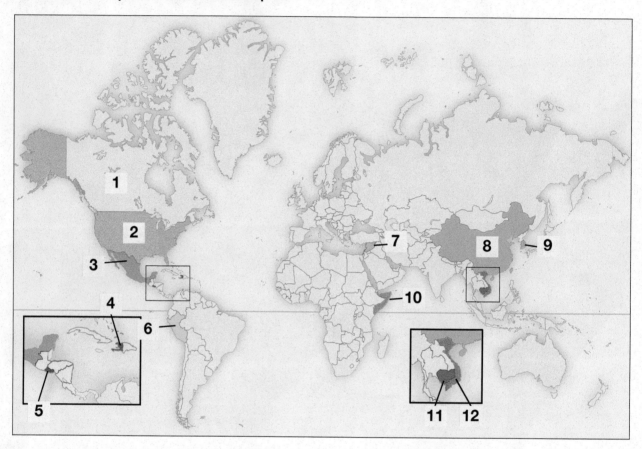

B ▶ Listen and read. Listen and repeat.

1. Canada	**2.** the United States	**3.** Mexico
4. Haiti	**5.** El Salvador	**6.** Peru
7. Syria	**8.** China	**9.** South Korea
10. Somalia	**11.** Cambodia	**12.** Vietnam

C **MAKE CONNECTIONS.** Point to your native country. Say the name.

Introduce Yourself

2 CONVERSATION

A ▶ **Listen. Listen and repeat.**

A: Hello. My name is Rick Soto.
B: Hi. I'm May Chen.
A: Where are you from, May?
B: I'm from China.

B **Practice the conversation.**

C **WORK TOGETHER. Make new conversations.**

A: Hello. My name is _____.
B: Hi. I'm _____.
A: Where are you from, _____?
B: I'm from _____.

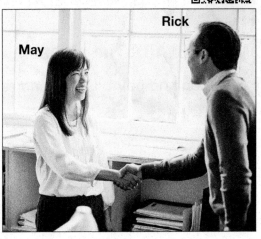

May

Rick

Show what you know!

1. TALK ABOUT IT. Make new conversations. Talk to three classmates.

What's your name?
Where are you from?

2. WRITE ABOUT IT. Write the names and countries.

Name	Country
1. May	China
2. _____	_____
3. _____	_____
4. _____	_____

I can introduce myself. ■   I need more practice. ■

Spell First and Last Names

What's your name?

1 VOCABULARY: The alphabet

A ▶ Listen and point. Listen and repeat.

Aa	Bb	Cc	Dd	Ee
Ff	Gg	Hh	Ii	Jj	Kk
Ll	Mm	Nn	Oo	Pp
Qq	Rr	Ss	Tt	Uu
Vv	Ww	Xx	Yy	Zz

B ▶ Listen. Write capital letters.

1. _____   2. _____   3. _____
4. _____   5. _____   6. _____
7. _____   8. _____   9. _____
10. _____   11. _____   12. _____

> B—capital letter
> b—lowercase letter

C WORK TOGETHER. Say a letter. Write the letter.

_____ _____ _____ _____ _____ _____

D ▶ Listen. Write the words.

1. _____   2. _____
3. _____   4. _____
5. _____   6. _____

Spell First and Last Names

2 CONVERSATION

A ▶ Listen. Listen and repeat.

A: What's your name, please?
B: Ana Sol.
A: Spell your first name.
B: A-N-A.
A: Spell your last name.
B: S-O-L.

B Practice the conversation.

Ana

Show what you know!

1. TALK ABOUT IT. Make new conversations. Talk to three classmates.

A: What's your name, please?
B: _____
A: Spell your first name.
B: _____
A: Spell your last name.
B: _____

2. WRITE ABOUT IT. Complete the chart.

First Name	Last Name
1. Ana	Sol
2.	
3.	
4.	

I can spell first and last names. ■   I need more practice. ■

Say and Write Important Numbers

What's your phone number?

1 VOCABULARY: Numbers 0–9

A ▶ Listen and point. Listen and repeat.

0	1	2	3	4	5	6	7	8	9
zero	one	two	three	four	five	six	seven	eight	nine

B ▶ Listen. Write the numbers.

a. _____ b. _____ c. _____ d. _____ e. _____ f. _____

C ▶ Listen. Circle the student ID.

1.

STUDENT ID
Name: **John Pace**
ID number: **02468**

STUDENT ID
Name: **John Potter**
ID number: **01469**

2.

STUDENT ID
Name: **Sue Gao**
ID number: **78396**

STUDENT ID
Name: **Grace Tang**
ID number: **65378**

3.

STUDENT ID
Name: **Anne Joseph**
ID number: **05376**

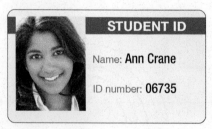

STUDENT ID
Name: **Ann Crane**
ID number: **06735**

Say and Write Important Numbers

2 CONVERSATION

A ▶ Listen. Listen and repeat.

A: What's your student ID number?
B: 83241.
A: 83241?
B: That's right.

B Practice the conversation.

C ▶ Listen. Listen and repeat.

A: What's your phone number?
B: 212-555-7169.
A: 212-555-7169?
B: That's right.

D Practice the conversation.

E ▶ Listen. Circle the phone number.

1. 231-555-3287   231-555-7283

2. 434-555-0516   434-555-1065

F ▶ Listen. Write the phone number.

1. _____ _____ _____ - _____ _____ _____ - _____ _____ _____ _____

2. _____ _____ _____ - _____ _____ _____ - _____ _____ _____ _____

3. _____ _____ _____ - _____ _____ _____ - _____ _____ _____ _____

Show what you know!

1. TALK ABOUT IT. Say a phone number.

917-555-9546

2. WRITE ABOUT IT. Write the number your partner says.

_____

I can say and write important numbers. ■   I need more practice. ■

Talk About Yourself

Nice to meet you.

1 **GRAMMAR:** *I am, you are*

I am Dana.
I'm Dana.
I'm a student.

You are Martin.
You're Martin.
You're a teacher.

A Write *am* or *are*.

1. I _____*am*_____ a student.
2. You _____ the teacher.
3. You _____ from Peru.
4. I _____ from the United States.
5. I _____ from Syria.
6. You _____ my classmate.

I am = I'm
you are = you're

B Rewrite the sentences in Exercise A. Use *I'm* and *You're*.

1. *I'm a student.* _____
2. _____
3. _____
4. _____
5. _____
6. _____

C ▶ Listen and check your answers. Listen and repeat.

Talk About Yourself

2 CONVERSATION

A ▶ Listen. Listen and repeat.

A: Hello. I'm Rosa.
B: Hi. I'm Rick. Nice to meet you.
A: Nice to meet you, too.

B Practice the conversation.

Rick

Rosa

Show what you know!

1. TALK ABOUT IT. Introduce yourself to your classmates.

A: Hello. I'm _____.
B: Hi. I'm _____. Nice to meet you.
A: Nice to meet you, too.

2. WRITE ABOUT IT. Write the names.

_____   _____

_____   _____

_____   _____

_____   _____

I can talk about myself. ■   I need more practice. ■

Introduce Someone
Jin Su is from Korea.

1 VOCABULARY: *He, she*

A ▶ Listen and point. Listen and repeat.

He is a student.

She is a teacher.

B Write *he* or *she*.

1. _____

2. _____

3. _____

4. _____

5. _____

6. _____

2 CONVERSATION

A ▶ Listen. Listen and repeat.

A: This is Jin Su. He is from Korea.
B: Hi, Jin Su. I'm Lora.
C: Nice to meet you.
B: Nice to meet you, too.

B Practice the conversation.

Jin Su   Lora

Introduce Someone

3 GRAMMAR: *He is, she is*

Jin Su **is** from Korea.
He is from Korea.
He's from Korea.

Lora **is** from the United States.
She is from the United States.
She's from the United States.

he is = he's
she is = she's

Write three sentences for each picture. Use *he*, *she*, *he's*, or *she's*.

1.  Carla / from Chile.

Carla is from Chile.
She is from Chile.
She's from Chile.

2. Sara / from Somalia

_____

_____

_____

3. Fang / a student

_____

_____

_____

4. Mr. Lane / a teacher

_____

_____

_____

Show what you know!

1. TALK ABOUT IT. Introduce classmates.

A: This is _____. _____ is from _____.
B: Hi, _____. I'm _____.
C: Nice to meet you.
B: Nice to meet you, too.

2. WRITE ABOUT IT. Write the names.

I can introduce someone. ■

I need more practice. ■

Lesson 6 | Talk About People

Who are they?

1 VOCABULARY: *You, we, they*

▶ Listen and point. Listen and repeat.

You are from Bolivia.

We are classmates.

They are students.

2 CONVERSATION

A ▶ Listen. Listen and repeat.

A: Who are they?
B: Oscar and Carlos. They're my classmates.
A: Where are they from?
B: They're from Brazil.

B Practice the conversation.

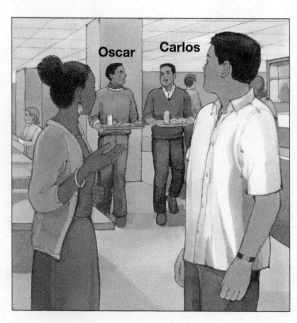

Oscar   Carlos

Talk About People

3 GRAMMAR: *You are, we are, they are*

You and Su **are** from China.	Tim and I **are** from Peru.	Joan and Kim **are** students.
You are from China.	**We are** from Peru.	**They are** students.
You're from China.	**We're** from Peru.	**They're** students.

Write three sentences. Use *you, we, they* and *you're, we're, they're*.

> you are = you're
> we are = we're
> they are = they're

1. Carlo and Ana / from Brazil

<u>Carlo and Ana are from Brazil.</u>

<u>They are from Brazil.</u>

_____

2. Mr. Edison and you / good teachers

_____

_____

_____

3. Edna and I / from Haiti

_____

_____

_____

Show what you know!

1. WRITE ABOUT IT. Write two sentences about your classmates.

_____ and _____ are _____.

They are _____.

2. TELL THE CLASS. Read your sentences.

Dan and Ana are students. They are from Haiti.

I can talk about people. ■	I need more practice. ■

Lesson 7

Joe is a student.

1 READING

A ▶ Listen and read.

Adult Education Center

First Name	Middle Name	Last Name
Joe	Lee	Baker

Phone Number	Place of Birth
760-555-7765	Canada

Student ID Number
78031

B Read the form again. Circle *Yes* or *No*.

1. This is Joe's form.   Yes   No
2. His middle name is Baker.   Yes   No
3. His last name is Lee.   Yes   No
4. Joe is a student.   Yes   No
5. He is from China.   Yes   No
6. His phone number is 7765.   Yes   No
7. Joe's student ID number is 78031.   Yes   No

C WORK TOGETHER. Compare your answers.

2 WRITING

A Complete the sentences.

1. My first name is _____.
2. My last name is _____.
3. My phone number is _____.
4. I'm from _____.
5. My student ID number is _____.

B Fill out the form. Use your information in Exercise A.

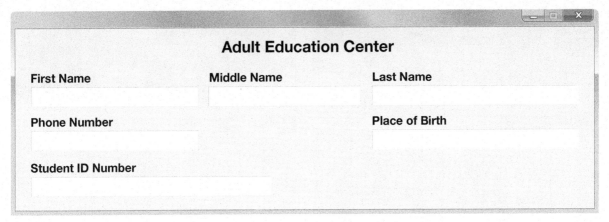

Adult Education Center

First Name | Middle Name | Last Name

Phone Number | Place of Birth

Student ID Number

C WORK TOGETHER. Read your classmate's form. Is the form complete?

D GO ONLINE.

1. Find your school's website.
2. Write the school's phone number.

_____

I can read and fill out a form. ■   I need more practice. ■

Read and Write About Greetings

This is Ivan.

1 LISTENING

A Look at each picture. What do you see?

B ▶ Listen to the story.

Read and Write About Greetings

2 READING

A ▶ Read and listen.

This is Ivan. He is a student.
He says hello to his classmates and smiles.
In his school, some students say hello and shake hands.
Some students say hello and hug.
Some students say hello and bow.
Other students say hello and kiss.

B Circle *Yes* or *No*.

1. Ivan says hello.   Yes   No
2. Ivan smiles.   Yes   No
3. Ivan hugs.   Yes   No
4. Some students bow.   Yes   No
5. Ivan shakes hands.   Yes   No

3 WRITING

A MAKE CONNECTIONS. Talk about people in your native country.

1. Do they say hello and smile?
2. Do they shake hands?
3. Do they hug?
4. Do they bow?
5. Do they kiss?

B Complete the sentences.

1. In my native country, some people say hello and _____.
2. Other people say hello and _____.
3. In my school, some students say hello and _____.
4. Other students say hello and _____.

C WORK TOGETHER. Read your sentences.

I can read and write about greetings. ■   I need more practice. ■

English at Work: Say Hello

Sam is at work.

Sam   Customer

1 READING

Sam is a greeter.
He works in a store.
He says hello to customers.

2 CONVERSATION AT WORK

A Complete the conversation. Write the correct words.

Sam: _____ to Buy Best.

Customer: _____.

Sam: Can I help you?

Customer: No _____. I'm fine.

Welcome	Hello
Thank you	You're welcome
hello	thank you

B Practice the conversation.

C Role-play the conversation with new information.

I can say hello. ■   I need more practice. ■

VOCABULARY REVIEW

A ▶ **LISTEN.** Listen and repeat.

Cambodia	eight	first name	five
hug	kiss	last name	nine
phone number	place of birth	shake hands	smile
Somalia	three	the United States	Vietnam

B Complete the chart. Use the words in Exercise A.

Countries	Ways to Say Hello	Numbers	Words on a Form

C Write *he*, *she*, or *they*.

1. _____

2. _____

3. _____

GRAMMAR REVIEW

A Complete the sentences. Write *am*, *is,* or *are*.

1. We _____*are*_____ teachers.
2. He _____ from China.
3. They _____ from Vietnam.
4. She _____ a teacher.
5. I _____ Lily.
6. You _____ from Canada.
7. I _____ a teacher.
8. You _____ students.
9. She _____ from Peru.
10. We _____ from Mexico.
11. He _____ a student.

B Rewrite the sentences from Exercise A. Use contractions.

1. *We're teachers.* _____
2. _____
3. _____
4. _____
5. _____
6. _____
7. _____
8. _____
9. _____
10. _____
11. _____

ROLE-PLAY.

A Introduce yourself.

A: Hello. I'm _____. What's your name?

B: Hi. I'm _____. Nice to meet you.

A: Nice to meet you, too.

B: Where are you from?

A: I'm from _____. Where are you from?

B: I'm from _____.

B Walk around the room. Practice the conversation with more classmates.

LIFE SKILLS AND WRITING REVIEW

1 | LIFE SKILLS: Read a form

ABC English Center
Student Information Form

First Name	Middle Name	Last Name
Marta		Cruz

Phone Number	Place of Birth
202-555-1234	El Salvador

Student ID Number
63588

Answer the questions.

1. What is the student's first name? _____
2. What is the student's last name? _____
3. What is her phone number? _____
4. Where is she from? _____
5. What is her student ID number? _____

2 | WRITE ABOUT YOURSELF

Fill out the form. Use your information.

ABC English Center
Student Information Form

First Name _____   Middle Name _____   Last Name _____

Phone Number _____   Place of Birth _____

Student ID Number _____

Unit Review: Go back to page 5. Which unit goals can you check off?

2 Welcome to Class

PREVIEW

Look at the picture. Who do you see?
What are they doing?

UNIT GOALS

- ☐ Ask for things in class
- ☐ Follow classroom instructions
- ☐ Talk about places in a school
- ☐ Describe locations
- ☐ Talk about study skills
- ☐ Read and write about classrooms
- ☐ **Life skills:** Understand a form
- ☐ **English at work:** Help someone fill out a form

Ask for Things in Class

Do you have a pen?

1 VOCABULARY: Classroom items

A Look at the pictures. What do you see?

1

2

3

4

5

6

7

8

9

B ▶ Listen and read. Listen and repeat.

1. a dictionary app	**2.** a pen	**3.** a book
4. an eraser	**5.** a piece of paper	**6.** a phone
7. a notebook	**8.** a pencil	**9.** a backpack

C MAKE CONNECTIONS. Look around the classroom. What do you see?

Ask for Things in Class

2 CONVERSATION

A ▶ **Listen. Listen and repeat.**

A: Excuse me. Do you have a pencil?
B: No, I don't.
A: Do you have a pen?
B: Yes, I do. Here you go.
A: Thanks.

B Practice the conversation.

C **WORK TOGETHER.** Make new conversations.

A: Excuse me. Do you have _____?
B: No, I don't.
A: Do you have _____?
B: Yes, I do. Here you go.
A: Thanks.

Show what you know!

1. **WRITE ABOUT IT.** What do you have? Write classroom objects.

_____ *a book* _____   _____

_____   _____

_____   _____

2. **TELL THE CLASS.** What do you have? Tell your classmates.

I have a book and a pen.

I can ask for things in class. ■   I need more practice. ■

Lesson 2

Please close your books.

1 VOCABULARY: Classroom instructions

A Look at the pictures. What do you see?

B Watch and listen to your teacher.

C ▶ Listen and read. Listen and repeat.

1. Turn on the light.	**2.** Take out your pencil.	**3.** Open your book.
4. Close your book.	**5.** Put away your book.	**6.** Turn off the light.

D WORK TOGETHER. Student A: Say a classroom instruction. Student B: Point to the picture. Take turns.

Follow Classroom Instructions

2 CONVERSATION

A ▶ Listen. Listen and repeat.

A: It is time for a test. Please close your books.
B: OK.
A: Use a pencil. Don't use a pen.

B Practice the conversation.

3 GRAMMAR: Imperatives

Use a pencil.	**Don't use** a pencil. **Do not use** a pencil.
Put away your books.	**Don't put away** your books. **Do not put away** your books.

A Write sentences with *don't*.

> do not = don't

1. Open your backpack. _Don't open your backpack._
2. Use a dictionary app. _____
3. Put away your notebook. _____
4. Turn off your phone. _____
5. Take out your book. _____
6. Close the door. _____

B ▶ Listen and check your answers. Listen and repeat.

Show what you know!

1. **TALK ABOUT IT.** Student A: Give an instruction. Student B: Do the action.

2. **WRITE ABOUT IT.** Write the instructions.

   Close your book.

I can follow classroom instructions. ☐   I need more practice. ☐

Talk About Places in a School

Where is the teacher?

1 VOCABULARY: Places in a school

A ▶ Listen and point. Listen and repeat.

B ▶ Listen and read. Listen and repeat.

1. library	**2.** office	**3.** testing room
4. cafeteria	**5.** restroom	**6.** classroom
7. bookstore	**8.** computer lab	

C Write the places in your school.

_____office_____   _____   _____

_____   _____   _____

D **WORK TOGETHER.** Show your partner your words. Add more words.

Talk About Places in a School

2 CONVERSATION

A ▶ Listen. Listen and repeat.

A: Where is the teacher?
B: He's in the library.

B Practice the conversation.

C Complete the conversations.

1.

A: Where is the teacher?
B: He's in the _____.

2.

A: Where is Sara?
B: She's in the _____.

3.

A: Where is your book?
B: It's in the _____.

4.

A: Where is your backpack?
B: It's in the _____.

D ▶ Listen and check your answers. Listen and repeat.

Show what you know!

1. WRITE ABOUT IT. Make a new conversation.

A: Where is _____?
B: _____ is in the _____. Where is _____?
A: _____ is in the _____.

2. TALK ABOUT IT. Practice your conversation.

| I can talk about places in a school. ☐ | I need more practice. ☐ |

Describe Locations

Where is the library?

1 VOCABULARY: *Next to*

▶ **Listen and point. Listen and repeat.**

The bookstore is **next to** the testing room.
The testing room is **next to** the bookstore.

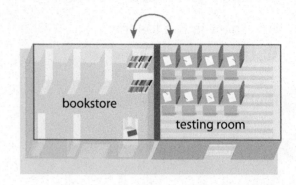

2 CONVERSATION

A ▶ **Listen. Listen and repeat.**

A: Excuse me. Where is the bookstore?
B: It's next to the testing room.
A: Thanks.

B **Practice the conversation.**

C **WORK TOGETHER.** Look at the pictures. Make new conversations. Use *next to*.

Conversation 1

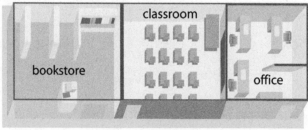

Conversation 2

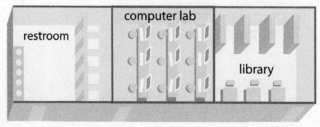

A: Excuse me. Where is the _____?
B: It's next to the _____.
A: Thanks.

Describe Locations

3 VOCABULARY: *Across from*

▶ Listen and point. Listen and repeat.

The library is **across from** the office.
The office is **across from** the library.

4 CONVERSATION

A ▶ Listen. Listen and repeat.

A: Excuse me. Where is the library?
B: It's across from the office.
A: Thanks.

B Practice the conversation.

C **WORK TOGETHER.**
Look at the picture.
Make new conversations.
Use *across from*.

A: Excuse me. Where is the
_____?
B: It's across from the
_____.
A: Thanks.

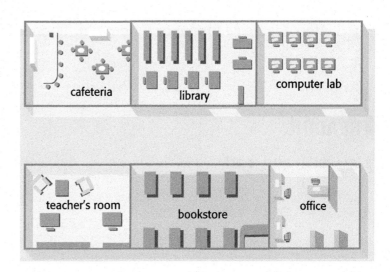

Show what you know!

1. WRITE ABOUT IT. Write about places in your school.

The _____ is next to the _____.
The _____ is across from the _____.

2. TALK ABOUT IT. Talk about the places.

The library is next to the office.

I can describe locations. ■   I need more practice. ■

Life Skills: Understand a Form

What's your first name?

1 VOCABULARY

Ⓐ ▶ Listen and repeat.

Mr.　　Mrs.　Ms.

married

Miss　　Ms.　　　Mr.

single

male

female

Ⓑ ▶ Listen. Circle *M* (male) or *F* (female). Then listen and repeat.

1.　　M　F　　　　2.　　M　F
3.　　M　F　　　　4.　　M　F

2 READING

Ⓐ ▶ Listen and read.

Vista Learning Center

○ Mr.

◉ Mrs.　　**Last Name**　　　　**First Name**
　　　　　Lopez　　　　　　　Alexa

○ Miss　　**Place of Birth**

○ Ms.　　　Mexico　　　◉ Female ○ Male

　　　　　Class　　　　　　**Teacher**
　　　　　English 100　　　　Mr. Chen

Ⓑ Read the form again. Circle *Yes* or *No*.

1. Alexa is married.　　　　　　　　Yes　　No
2. Alexa is from England.　　　　　　Yes　　No
3. Alexa is male.　　　　　　　　　　Yes　　No
4. Alexa is in English 100.　　　　　　Yes　　No
5. Alexa's teacher is Mr. Lopez.　　　Yes　　No

3 WRITING

A Answer the questions.

1. What is your first name? _____

2. What is your last name? _____

3. What class are you in? _____

4. What is your teacher's name? _____

5. Where are you from? _____

B Fill out the form. Use your information in Exercise A.

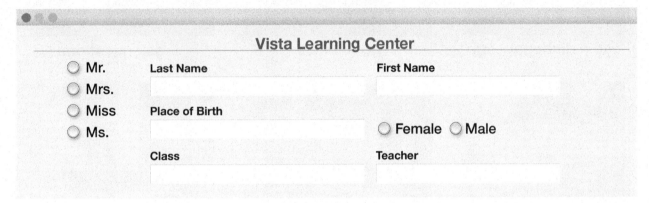

C **WORK TOGETHER.** Read your classmate's form. Is the form complete?

D GO ONLINE.

1. Find a form online.

2. Fill out the form with your information.

I can understand a form. ■   I need more practice. ■

Lesson 6 How do you study English?

1 VOCABULARY: Study skills

▶ Listen and point. Listen and repeat.

use a dictionary app

go to class

ask questions

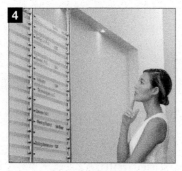
read signs

write new words

practice with my classmates

2 CONVERSATION

A ▶ Listen. Listen and repeat.

A: How do you study English?
B: I practice with my classmates, and I write new words.
A: That's great!

B Practice the conversation.

C **WORK TOGETHER.** Make new conversations.

A: How do you study English?
B: I _____, and I _____.

Talk About Study Skills

3 GRAMMAR: Simple present: *I, you, we, they*

I practice with my classmates.	**We write** new words.
You use a dictionary app.	**They ask** questions.

A Complete the paragraph. Use words from the box.

Rosa

go	practice	read	~~study~~	use	write

My name is Rosa. I _____*study*_____ English. I _____
to class every day. I _____ English with my
classmates. We _____ new words in our notebooks. I _____
a dictionary app on my phone. On the street, I _____ signs. How do you
study English?

B Complete the sentences. Use words from the box.

go	practice	read	write

1. I _____ to class every day.

2. They _____ signs on the street.

3. We _____ with our classmates.

4. You _____ new words.

Show what you know!

1. TALK ABOUT IT. Ask your classmates: *How do you study English?*
Check (✓) the boxes.

☐ go to class   ☐ write new words
☐ ask questions   ☐ use a dictionary app
☐ practice with my classmates   ☐ read signs

2. WRITE ABOUT IT. Write sentences.

We ask questions. We read signs.

I can talk about study skills. ■	I need more practice. ■

Read and Write About Classrooms

This is Lan.

1 LISTENING

A Look at each picture. What do you see?

B ▶ Listen to the story.

Read and Write About Classrooms

2 READING

A ▶ Read and listen.

This is Lan.
In her native country, students do not talk in class.
They listen to the teacher.
In the United States, students talk in groups.
Students ask questions.
The teacher listens to the students.

B Circle *Yes* or *No*.

1. Lan is from the United States.	Yes	No
2. In Lan's native country, students talk in class.	Yes	No
3. In the United States, students ask questions.	Yes	No
4. In the United States, the teacher listens to the students.	Yes	No

3 WRITING

A MAKE CONNECTIONS. Talk about students in your native country.

1. Do students talk in class?
2. Do students ask questions in class?

B Complete the sentences.

1. In my native country, students _____ in class.
2. They _____ in class.
3. In the United States, students _____ in class.
4. They _____ in class.

C WORK TOGETHER. Read your sentences.

I can read and write about classrooms. ■	I need more practice. ■

English at Work: Help Someone Fill Out a Form

Alma is at work.

Alma

Student

1 READING

Alma is a secretary.
She works in a school.
She helps a student fill out a form.

2 CONVERSATION AT WORK

A Complete the conversation. Write the correct words.

Alma: What is your _____?

Student: My last _____ is Sanchez.

Alma: OK. What is your _____
name?

Student: My _____ is Rosa.
My name is Rosa Sanchez.

Alma: Great! Write your first and last name on the form here.

classroom	last name
name	teacher
first	school
teacher's name	first name

B Practice the conversation.

C Role-play the conversation with your information.

I can help someone fill out a form. ☐   I need more practice. ☐

VOCABULARY REVIEW

A ▶ **LISTEN.** Listen and repeat.

book	cafeteria	close	computer lab	library
notebook	office	open	pen	pencil
put away	restroom	take out	turn on	

B Write the words.

   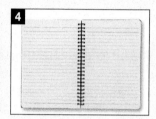

1. _____ 2. _____ 3. _____ 4. _____

 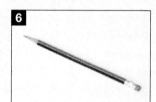  

5. _____ 6. _____ 7. _____ 8. _____

C Complete the chart. Use the words in Exercise A.

Classroom Items	Places in a School	Classroom Instructions

GRAMMAR REVIEW

A Write sentences.

1. *Open your book.*   Don't open your book.
2. Use a dictionary app.   _____
3. Turn on your phone.   _____
4. _____ Don't open the door.
5. Turn off the light.   _____
6. _____ Don't put away your notebook.

B Complete the sentences. Use words from the box.

ask	eat	go	~~study~~	talk	use	write

1. I _____ study _____ English.
2. We _____ in groups.
3. We _____ to school every day.
4. They _____ in the cafeteria.
5. I _____ a dictionary app on my phone.
6. They _____ in their notebooks.
7. I _____ questions in the classroom.

C How do you study? Write sentences. Use words from the box.

ask questions	read signs
~~go to class~~	use a dictionary app
practice with my friends	write new words

I go to class. _____

_____

_____

_____

_____

_____

ROLE-PLAY.

Student A
Ask about places in the school.

Student B
Help Student A. Look at the map.
Use *across from* or *next to*.

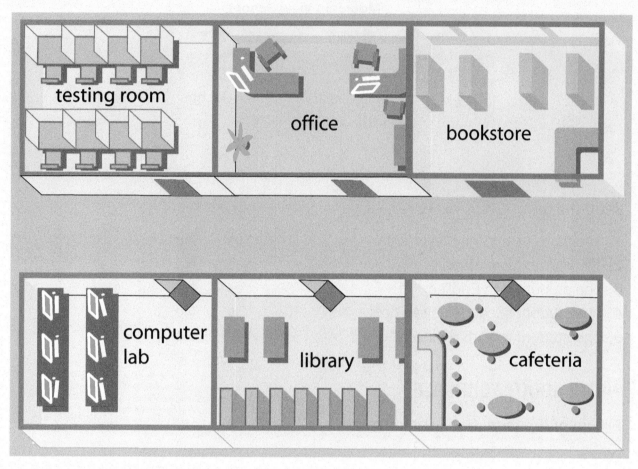

A: Excuse me. Where is the _____?

B: It's next to the _____.

A: Thanks.

Switch roles.

B: Excuse me. Where is the _____?

A: It's across from the _____.

B: Thanks.

LIFE SKILLS AND WRITING REVIEW

1 LIFE SKILLS: Understand a form

Student Information Form
Mountain View School

○ Mr.
● Mrs.
○ Miss
○ Ms.

Last Name	First Name
Antar	Haya

Class	Teacher
English 101	Mr. Jacobs

Place of Birth
Syria

Read the form. Circle *Yes* or *No*.

1. The student's first name is Antar.   Yes   No
2. The student is married.   Yes   No
3. The student is in English 101.   Yes   No
4. The student's teacher is Mr. Antar.   Yes   No
5. The student is from Syria.   Yes   No

2 WRITE ABOUT YOURSELF

Fill out of the form. Use your information.

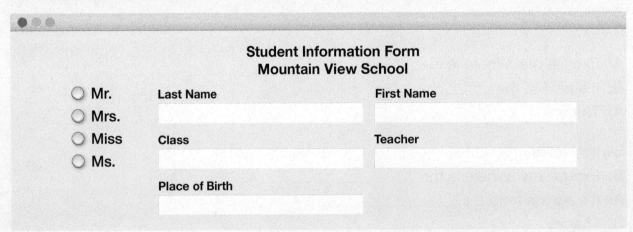

Student Information Form
Mountain View School

○ Mr.
○ Mrs.
○ Miss
○ Ms.

Last Name	First Name

Class	Teacher

Place of Birth

Unit Review: Go back to page 27. Which unit goals can you check off?

3 On Time

PREVIEW

Look at the picture. Who do you see?
What is he doing?

UNIT GOALS

- Say the time
- Talk about schedules
- Talk about daily activities
- Talk about your weekly schedule
- Read and write about time

- **Life skills:** Read and write a weekly schedule
- **English at work:** Talk about schedules

Say the Time

What time is it?

1 VOCABULARY: Numbers and time

A Look at the numbers.

▶ Listen and point. Listen and repeat.

0	1	2	3	4	5	6	7	8	9
10	11	12	13	14	15	16	17	18	19

20	21	22	23	24	25	26	27	28	29
30	31	32	33	34	35	36	37	38	39

40	41	42	43	44	45	46	47	48	49
50	51	52	53	54	55	56	57	58	59

B WORK TOGETHER. Point to a number. Say the number.

C ▶ Listen. Circle the number.

a. 10	20		**b.** 17	19
c. 24	14		**d.** 30	13
e. 15	50		**f.** 42	14
g. 26	36		**h.** 27	47

D ▶ Listen and point. Listen and repeat.

1. 1:00
2. 1:05
3. 1:15
4. 1:20

5. 1:30
6. 1:40
7. 1:45
8. 1:50

2 CONVERSATION

A ▶ Listen. Listen and repeat.

A: What time is it?

B: It's 1:00.

B Practice the conversation.

C Write the times.

1. _____   2. _____   3. _____   4. _____

5. _____   6. _____   7. _____   8. _____

D WORK TOGETHER. Point to the times. Make new conversations.

Show what you know!

TALK ABOUT IT. What time is it? Ask and answer. Take turns.

A: What time is it?

B: It's 8:05.

| I can say the time. ■ | I need more practice. ■ |

What time is your break?

1 VOCABULARY: Talking about times

▶ Listen and point. Listen and repeat.

Class **is at** 9:00.

Class **is over at** 12:30.

My break is **from** 10:45 **to** 11:15.

2 CONVERSATION

A ▶ Listen. Listen and repeat.

A: What time is your English class?
B: It's from 9:00 to 12:30.
A: What time is your break?
B: It's from 10:45 to 11:15.

B Circle *Yes* or *No*.

1. The class is at 9:00.   Yes   No
2. The class is over at 12:00.   Yes   No
3. The break is at 10:45.   Yes   No

C Practice the conversation.

D WORK TOGETHER. Make new conversations.

A: What time is your English class?
B: It's from _____ to _____.
A: What time is your break?
B: It's from _____ to _____.

Talk About Schedules

3 GRAMMAR: *From / to, at*

My class is **from** 9:00 **to** 12:30.

My break is **from** 10:45 **to** 11:15.

My class is **at** 9:00.
My class is over **at** 12:30.

My break is **at** 10:45.
My break is over **at** 11:15.

A Complete the sentences. Use *from, to,* or *at.*

1. My English class is _____*at*_____ 1:00.
2. Lunch is _____ 12:00 _____ 1:00.
3. Our class is _____ 4:30.
4. His work day is over _____ 5:00.
5. Ella's break is _____ 3:15 _____ 3:30.

B Write sentences. Use *from, to,* or *at.*

1. Lunch is / 11:00 / 11:45   *Lunch is from 11:00 to 11:45.* _____
2. English class is / 6:30   _____
3. The break is / 8:00 / 8:15   _____
4. Our class is over / 9:30   _____
5. Her class is / 2:00 / 3:30   _____

Show what you know!

1. WRITE ABOUT IT. What is your class or work schedule?

My _____ is from _____ to _____.
My break is at _____. It is over at _____.

2. TELL THE CLASS. Talk about your class or work schedule.

My English class is from 9:00 to 11:30.
My break is at 10:30. It is over at 10:45.

I can talk about schedules. ■   I need more practice. ■

Talk About Daily Activities

What time do you go to work?

1 VOCABULARY: Daily activities

A Look at the pictures. What do you see?

▶ Listen and point. Listen and repeat.

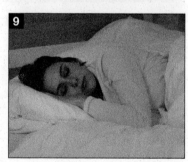

B ▶ Listen and read. Listen and repeat.

1. get up	**2.** take a shower	**3.** get dressed
4. eat breakfast	**5.** go to work	**6.** eat lunch
7. go to school	**8.** get home	**9.** go to sleep

C Answer the questions.

1. What time do you get up? _I get up at 6:30._
2. What time do you eat lunch? _____
3. What time do you get home? _____
4. What time do you go to sleep? _____

Talk About Daily Activities

2 CONVERSATION

A ▶ Listen. Listen and repeat.

A: What time do you go to work?
B: I go to work at 6:00. What time do you go to work?
A: I go to work at 10:00.

B Practice the conversation.

C WORK TOGETHER. Make new conversations.

A: What time do you _____?
B: I _____ at _____.
   What time do you _____?
A: I _____ at _____.

Show what you know!

1. WRITE ABOUT IT. What time do you do things? Write times.

I get up _____.
I eat breakfast _____.
I go to work _____.
I go to school _____.
I get home _____.
I go to sleep _____.

2. TALK ABOUT IT. Ask and answer questions.

A: What time do you get up?
B: I get up at 6:00.

I can talk about daily activities. ■   I need more practice. ■

1 VOCABULARY: Days of the week

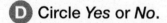 Listen and point. Listen and repeat.

Sunday	Monday	Tuesday	Wednesday	Thursday	Friday	Saturday
go to library	work	work	work	work	work	school

> Start days of the week with a capital letter.

2 CONVERSATION

A ▶ Listen. Listen and repeat.

A: When do you work, Nora?
B: I work from Monday to Friday.
A: When do you go to school?
B: I go to school on Saturday.
A: You're really busy!

Nora

B Practice the conversation.

C ▶ Listen and read.

Hi, I'm Nora. I'm very busy. I work from Monday to Friday. I go to school on Saturday. I go to the library on Sunday.

D Circle *Yes* or *No*.

1. Nora works from Monday to Friday.   Yes   No
2. She goes to school on Sunday.   Yes   No
3. She works on Wednesday.   Yes   No
4. She goes to the library on Saturday.   Yes   No

Talk About Your Weekly Schedule

3 GRAMMAR: *From / to, on*

I work **from** Monday **to** Friday.	I go to school **on** Monday and Wednesday.

A Complete the sentences. Use *from, to,* or *on*.

1. I work _____*from*_____ Monday _____*to*_____ Thursday.
2. We play soccer _____ Tuesday.
3. I go to school _____ Friday.
4. They go to school _____ Wednesday _____ Friday.
5. I eat lunch at home _____ Sunday.

B ▶ Listen and check your answers. Listen and repeat.

Show what you know!

1. WRITE ABOUT IT. Write your weekly schedule.

	Sunday	Monday	Tuesday	Wednesday	Thursday	Friday	Saturday
work							
school							

2. TALK ABOUT IT. Talk about your weekly schedule.

I work from Tuesday to Saturday. I go to school on Monday.

I can talk about my weekly schedule. ☐	I need more practice. ☐

Life Skills: Read and Write a Weekly Schedule

Felipe works on Monday and Tuesday.

1 READING

A Read Felipe's weekly schedule.

SUN	10:30–1:00 study
	1:00–10:00 rest!
MON	9:00–5:00 work
	12:00–12:45 break
TUE	8:30–2:00 school
WED	9:00–5:00 work
	12:00–12:45 break
THU	10:30–3:00 school
	6:00–7:30 English class
FRI	9:30–2:30 work
	12:00–12:45 break
SAT	11:00–2:00 practice English

Felipe is **resting**.

B Complete the sentences.

1. Felipe works from _____ to _____ on Monday.
2. His break is from _____ to _____ on Monday, Wednesday, and _____.
3. Felipe goes to school from _____ to _____ on Tuesday.
4. He goes to school from 10:30 to 3:00 on _____.
5. He works from _____ to _____ on Friday.
6. He practices English from _____ to _____ on _____.
7. His English class is from _____ to _____ on _____.
8. Felipe rests from _____ to _____ on _____.

Life Skills: Read and Write a Weekly Schedule

2 WRITING

A Complete your weekly schedule.

B Answer the questions.

1. When do you work?

2. When do you go to school?

3. When do you practice English?

4. When do you study?

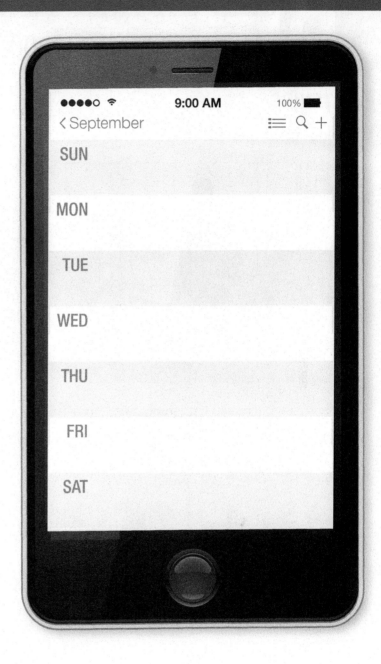

C GO ONLINE.

1. Find the class schedule for your school online.
2. Write sentences.

   English class is on Monday and Wednesday.

| I can read and write a weekly schedule. ☐ | I need more practice. ☐ |

Lesson 6

Read and Write About Time

Manny gets up at 6:00.

1 LISTENING

A Look at each picture. What do you see?

B ▶ Listen to the story.

Read and Write About Time

2 READING

A ▶ **Read and listen.**

Manny gets up at 6:00.
He gets to work at 7:55. He starts work at 8:00. He is on time.
He goes to school after work.
He gets to class at 5:45. Class starts at 6:00. He is early.
Manny meets friends on Saturday. But he is late!

B Circle *Yes* or *No*.

1.	Manny starts work at 7:00.	Yes	No
2.	He is late for work.	Yes	No
3.	Class starts at 6:45.	Yes	No
4.	Manny is early for class.	Yes	No
5.	He is late on Saturday.	Yes	No

3 WRITING

A **MAKE CONNECTIONS.** Talk about people in your native country.

1. Do people go to work on time?
2. Do people go to school on time?
3. Do people meet friends on time?

B Complete the sentences.

1. In my native country, people go to work _____.
2. They go to school _____.
3. They meet friends _____.

C **WORK TOGETHER.** Read your sentences.

I can read and write about time. ■   I need more practice. ■

Wei is at work.

Employee

Wei

1 READING

Wei is a manager.
He works in a supermarket.
He talks about his employee's schedule.

2 CONVERSATION AT WORK

A Complete the conversation. Write the correct words.

Wei:	It is 9:10. You're _____.	late	early
Employee:	_____!	I'm sorry	Thank you
Wei:	Work _____ at 9:00. Why are you late?	starts	stops
Employee:	The bus was _____. I'm sorry.	on time	late
Wei:	OK. Please call me next time.		

B Practice the conversation.

C Role-play the conversation with new information.

I can talk about schedules. ■   I need more practice. ■

VOCABULARY REVIEW

A ► **LISTEN. Write the numbers.**

1. _____   2. _____   3. _____   4. _____   5. _____

6. _____   7. _____   8. _____   9. _____   10. _____

B Look at the numbers in Exercise A. Write them in the correct order.

___   ___   ___   ___   ___   ___   ___   ___   ___   ___

C Write the days of the week in the correct order.

Friday   Monday   Saturday   Sunday   Thursday   Tuesday   Wednesday

1. _____   2. _____   3. _____

4. _____   5. _____   6. _____

7. _____

D Write the daily activities.

eat breakfast   get home   go to school   go to sleep   go to work   take a shower

1. _____

2. _____

3. _____

4. _____

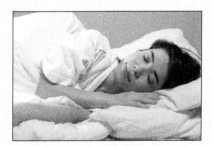

5. _____

6. _____

GRAMMAR REVIEW

A Complete the sentences. Use *from, to, at,* or *on.*

1. Class is _____ at _____ 8:00.

2. I work _____ Monday _____ Thursday.

3. Sal goes to work _____ 7:30.

4. Our break is _____ 3:00 _____ 3:15.

5. Dan goes to school _____ Monday and Wednesday.

6. Peter gets up _____ 8:30 _____ Saturday.

7. Min goes to sleep _____ 11:00 _____ Friday.

8. Sue works _____ 8:00 _____ 4:00.

9. We eat lunch _____ 12:00 _____ 1:00 every day.

10. Sam goes to work _____ 9:00 _____ Thursday.

B Write sentences. Use *from, to, at,* or *on.*

1. They work / Monday / Friday. _They work from Monday to Friday._

2. English class is / 5:00 _____

3. Class is over / 7:00 _____

4. I go to school / Saturday _____

5. They eat breakfast / 7:30 _____

6. Our break is / 12:15 / 12:30 _____

7. Kate and Joe work / 8:30 / 4:00 _____

8. I study / Saturday _____

9. I work / Tuesday / Friday _____

10. We work / 12:00 / 5:00 / Saturday _____

_____

ROLE-PLAY.

Student A
Ask about Student B's schedule.
Then answer Student B's questions.

Student B
Answer Student A's questions.
Then ask about Student A's schedule.

A: When do you work?

B: I work from _____ to _____.

A: When do you go to school?

B: I go to school on _____.

A: What time do you _____?

B: I _____ at _____.

Student A

My Schedule

Sunday	Monday	Tuesday	Wednesday	Thursday	Friday	Saturday
go to library 12:00	get up 7:00 work 9:00–5:00 play soccer 6:00–7:30	get up 6:00 work 8:30–4:30 go to school 6:00–8:00	get up 7:00 work 9:00–5:00	get up 7:00 work 9:00–5:00	get up 7:00 work 9:00–5:00	get up 9:00 go to school 12:00–3:00 meet friends 6:00 go to sleep 11:00

Student B

My Schedule

Sunday	Monday	Tuesday	Wednesday	Thursday	Friday	Saturday
get up 10:00 meet friends 12:00	get up 9:00 go to school 10:00–5:00	get up 6:00 work 8:00–4:00	get up 7:00 work 9:00–5:00	get up 7:00 work 9:00–5:00 play soccer 6:00–7:30	get up 8:00 work 10:00–4:00 go to school 6:00–8:00	get up 9:00 work 11:00–6:00 go to sleep 11:30

LIFE SKILLS AND WRITING REVIEW

1 LIFE SKILLS: Read and write a weekly schedule

A Ask and answer the questions.

1. When do you work?
2. When do you go to school?
3. When is your break?
4. When do you study English?
5. When do you meet friends?

B Write your information in the schedule.

My Schedule

Sunday	Monday	Tuesday	Wednesday	Thursday	Friday	Saturday

2 WRITE ABOUT YOURSELF

Complete the sentences.

1. I work _____.
2. I go to class _____.
3. My break is _____.
4. I study English _____.
5. I meet friends _____.

Unit Review: Go back to page 47. Which unit goals can you check off?

4 Family and Home

PREVIEW

Look at the picture. Who do you see?
Why are they together?

UNIT GOALS

- ☐ Identify family members
- ☐ Say who is in your family
- ☐ Talk about chores at home
- ☐ Say months of the year
- ☐ Write dates

- ☐ Read and write about home and work
- ☐ **Life skills:** Fill out a form
- ☐ **English at work:** Ask about someone's family

Identify Family Members

That's my brother.

1 VOCABULARY: Family members

A Look at the pictures. What do you see?

▶ Listen and point. Listen and repeat.

B ▶ Listen and read. Listen and repeat.

1. sister	**2.** brother	**3.** husband	**4.** wife
5. grandmother	**6.** grandfather	**7.** parents	**8.** father
9. mother	**10.** daughter	**11.** son	**12.** children

Identify Family Members

2 CONVERSATION

A ▶ Listen. Listen and repeat.

A: Who's that?
B: That's my brother.
A: What's his name?
B: Sam.
A: Who's that?
B: That's my sister.
A: What's her name?
B: Her name is Tina.

B Practice the conversation.

Show what you know!

1. TALK ABOUT IT. Show pictures of your family. Ask and answer.

A: Who's that?
B: That's my _____.
A: What's _____ name?
B: _____ name is _____.

2. WRITE ABOUT IT. Write the names of your family members.

My sister is Emma.
My mother is Angela.

I can identify family members. ■   I need more practice. ☐

Say Who Is in Your Family

I have two sisters and one brother.

1 CONVERSATION

A ▶ Listen. Listen and repeat.

A: Do you have any sisters or brothers?
B: Yes. I have two sisters and one brother.
A: That's nice. Do you have any children?
B: No, I don't.

B Circle *Yes* or *No*.

1. The woman has two sisters.	Yes	No
2. The woman has two brothers.	Yes	No
3. The woman has children.	Yes	No

C Practice the conversation.

2 READING

A ▶ Listen and read.

Pedro   Marta   Linda   Roberto

Tino   Ernesto   Ana

Hi, I'm Marta. This is my family. That's my husband. His name is Pedro. My parents are Linda and Roberto. I have two sons, Ernesto and Tino. I have one daughter. Her name is Ana.

B Complete the sentences about Marta's family.

1. Pedro is her _____.

2. Ana is her _____.

3. Linda is her _____.

4. Ernesto and Tino are her _____.

5. Roberto and Linda are her _____.

3 GRAMMAR: Singular and plural

A ▶ Listen and read. Listen and repeat.

Singular	Plural
one brother	two brothers
a sister	three sisters
one son	two sons
a daughter	three daughters
one parent	two parents
one child	two children

B Match.

_b_ **1.** my brother Tom and my brother Mark   **a.** my parents

____ **2.** my son and daughter   **b.** my brothers

____ **3.** my mother and father   **c.** my sisters

____ **4.** my sister Sue and my sister Mary   **d.** my children

Show what you know!

1. TALK ABOUT IT. Ask and answer.

A: Do you have any sisters or brothers?
B: _____.
A: Do you have any children?
B: _____.

2. WRITE ABOUT IT. Write sentences.

I have one brother.
I have two daughters.

I can say who is in my family. ■   I need more practice. ■

Do you vacuum?

1 VOCABULARY: Household chores

A Look at the pictures. What do you see?

▶ Listen and point. Listen and repeat.

B ▶ Listen and read. Listen and repeat.

1. do the laundry	**2.** wash the dishes	**3.** make dinner
4. clean the house	**5.** vacuum	**6.** take out the garbage

C What household chores do you do? Read the sentences. Circle *Yes* or *No*.

1. I vacuum.	Yes	No
2. I do the laundry.	Yes	No
3. I make dinner.	Yes	No
4. I wash the dishes.	Yes	No
5. I clean the house.	Yes	No
6. I take out the garbage.	Yes	No

Talk About Chores at Home

2 CONVERSATION

A ▶ **Listen. Listen and repeat.**

A: Do you vacuum?
B: Yes, I do.
A: Do you make dinner?
B: No, I don't.

B Practice the conversation.

3 GRAMMAR: *Yes / No* questions

Questions	Answers
Do you wash the dishes?	**Yes,** I do.
Do you clean the house?	**No,** I don't.
Do you vacuum?	**Yes,** I do.
Do you do the laundry?	**No,** I don't.

Write the questions.

> End a question with a question mark.

1. you / vacuum   *Do you vacuum?* _____
2. you / do the laundry   _____
3. you / make dinner   _____
4. you / wash the dishes _____
5. you / clean the house _____
6. you / take out the garbage _____

Show what you know!

1. TALK ABOUT IT. Ask about household chores.

A: Do you _____?
B: _____, I _____.

2. WRITE ABOUT IT. What chores do you do?

I do the dishes.
I clean the house.

I can talk about chores at home. ■   I need more practice. ■

Say Months of the Year

What's your favorite season?

1 VOCABULARY: Months and seasons

A ▶ Listen and point. Listen and repeat.

Months

January	February	March	April	May	June

July	August	September	October	November	December

B ▶ Listen. Circle the month.

1. November   December
2. July   June
3. October   November
4. January   July
5. March   May
6. August   April

> Start months with a capital letter.

C Look at the pictures. What do you see?

▶ Listen and point. Listen and repeat.

Seasons

spring   summer   fall   winter

Say Months of the Year

D Write the months.

Seasons in the United States			
Spring	**Summer**	**Fall**	**Winter**

2 CONVERSATION

A ▶ Listen. Listen and repeat.

A: What's your favorite season?

B: Summer.

A: That's nice. My favorite season is spring.

B Practice the conversation.

C WORK TOGETHER. Make new conversations.

A: What's your favorite season?

B: _____.

A: That's nice. My favorite season is _____.

Show what you know!

1. TALK ABOUT IT. What's your favorite month?

A: What's your favorite month?
B: My favorite month is _____.

2. WRITE ABOUT IT. What's your favorite season?

My favorite season is fall.

I can say months of the year. ☐   I need more practice. ☐

Lesson 5

What is today's date?

1 VOCABULARY: Dates

A Put the months in the correct order. Write the numbers. Then write the words.

___ November   ___ December   ___ January   ___ March

___ April   ___ July   ___ February   ___ August

___ October   ___ May   ___ September   ___ June

1. _____   7. _____

2. _____   8. _____

3. _____   9. _____

4. _____   10. _____

5. _____   11. _____

6. _____   12. _____

B ▶ Listen and point. Listen and repeat.

September 28, 1998	January 2, 2018	June 20, 2010
9/28/1998	1/2/2018	6/20/2010

April 19, 2008	December 22, 1987	March 15, 2025
4/19/2008	12/22/1987	3/15/2025

C Match the dates.

1. January 1, 2017   5/15/1993
2. April 12, 2020   5/31/2014
3. May 15, 1993   1/1/2017
4. August 27, 2000   8/27/2000
5. May 31, 2014   4/12/2020

D ▶ Listen. Circle the date.

1. 2/23/1994   3/23/1994
2. 7/14/2015   7/4/2015
3. 9/22/2009   9/2/2009
4. 1/29/2011   1/11/2019
5. 9/17/1974   9/7/1974

Write Dates

E Write the dates. Use numbers.

  1. September 2, 2010   _____

  2. April 12, 2013   _____

  3. May 21, 2012   _____

  4. September 2, 1999   _____

  5. October 7, 2021   _____

  6. July 30, 1988   _____

2 CONVERSATION

A ▶ Listen. Listen and repeat.

  A: What is today's date?

  B: April 9, 2019.

  A: Thanks.

B Practice the conversation.

C WORK TOGETHER. Make new conversations.

  A: What is today's date?

  B: _____.

  A: Thanks.

Show what you know!

  1. WRITE ABOUT IT. Write dates. Use words and numbers.

    February 28, 2019

    2/28/2019

  2. TELL THE CLASS. Look at your partner's dates. Say the dates.

I can write dates. ■   I need more practice. ■

6

Life Skills: Fill Out a Form

What is your teacher's name?

1 READING

A ▶ Listen and read.

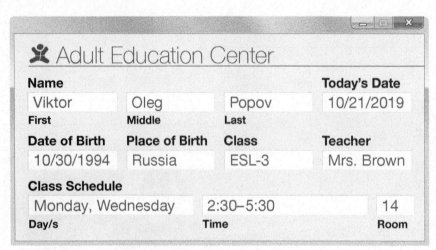

Adult Education Center

Name			Today's Date
Viktor	Oleg	Popov	10/21/2019
First	Middle	Last	

Date of Birth	Place of Birth	Class	Teacher
10/30/1994	Russia	ESL-3	Mrs. Brown

Class Schedule

Monday, Wednesday	2:30–5:30	14
Day/s	Time	Room

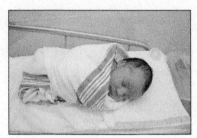

date of birth: 2/18/2019

B Complete the sentences about Viktor.

1. Viktor is a _____.
2. Viktor's last name is _____.
3. He is from _____.
4. Viktor's date of birth is _____.
5. His teacher is _____.
6. His class is _____.
7. His class is on Monday and _____.
8. His class is over at _____.

Life Skills: Fill Out a Form

2 WRITING

A Answer the questions.

1. What is your first name? _____
2. What is your last name? _____
3. What is your date of birth? _____
4. Where are you from? _____
5. What class are you in? _____
6. What is your teacher's name? _____
7. What day is your class? _____
8. What time does your class start? _____
9. What time does your class end? _____
10. What room is your class in? _____

B Fill out the form. Use your information in Exercise A.

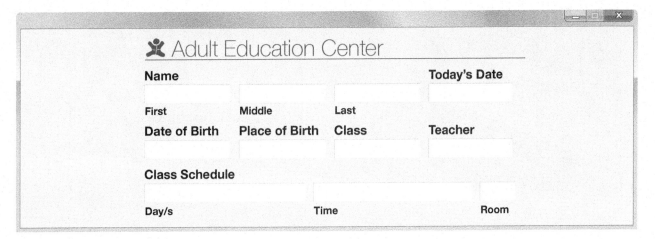

C WORK TOGETHER. Read your classmate's form. Is the form complete?

D GO ONLINE.

1. Find an application form online.
2. Fill out the form.

I can fill out a form. ☐   I need more practice. ☐

Lucas and Carla are married.

1 LISTENING

A Look at each picture. What do you see?

B ▶ Listen to the story.

Read and Write About Home and Work

2 READING

A ▶ **Read and listen.**

Lucas and Carla are married. Lucas is Carla's husband. Carla is Lucas's wife.
In their native country, men go to work.
In their native country, women do the household chores.
In the United States, Carla and Lucas go to work.
They both do household chores. Lucas washes the dishes.
Lucas goes to the supermarket, too.

B Circle *Yes* or *No*.

1. Lucas is Carla's husband.		Yes	No
2. In the United States, Carla goes to work.		Yes	No
3. In their native country, women go to work.		Yes	No
4. In the United States, Lucas does household chores.		Yes	No

3 WRITING

A **MAKE CONNECTIONS.** Talk about work and household chores in your native country.

1. Do men and women go to work?

2. Do women do household chores?

3. Do men do household chores? What household chores do they do?

B Complete the sentences.

1. In my native country, _____ work.

2. _____ do household chores.

3. In the United States, _____ work.

4. _____ do household chores.

C **WORK TOGETHER.** Read your sentences.

I can read and write about home and work. ■   I need more practice. ■

Mara is at work.

Mara

Co-worker

1 READING

Mara is an assistant.
She works in an office.
She asks her co-worker about her family.

2 CONVERSATION AT WORK

A Complete the conversation. Write the correct words.

Mara:	Is that your family?	
Co-worker:	Yes, it is. That's my _____ and three sisters.	brother sister
Mara:	_____?	That's nice Who's that
Co-worker:	That's my _____.	grandmother grandparents
Mara:	You have a nice family.	
Co-worker:	_____!	You're welcome Thank you

B Practice the conversation.

C Role-play the conversation with new information.

I can ask about someone's family. ■   I need more practice. ■

A Write the months of the year in the correct order.

1. _____   7. _____
2. _____   8. _____
3. _____   9. _____
4. _____   10. _____
5. _____   11. _____
6. _____   12. _____

B ▶ Listen and check your answers.

C Read the calendar. Write the dates in words and numbers.

April 5, 2020
4/5/2020

April 2020

S	M	T	W	T	F	S
			1	2	3	4
5	6	7	8	9	10	11
12	13	14	15	16	17	18
19	20	21	22	23	24	25
26	27	28	29	30		

D Write the chores.

clean the house   do the laundry   make dinner
take out the garbage   vacuum   wash the dishes

1. _____

2. _____

3. _____

4. _____

5. _____

6. _____

GRAMMAR REVIEW

A Complete the chart.

Singular	Plural
sister	sisters
parent	
	brothers
daughter	
	sons
grandmother	
child	

B Complete the conversations. Write *his* or *her*.

1. A: That's my brother.

   B: What's _____ his _____ name?

2. A: That's my grandmother.

   B: What's _____ name?

3. A: That's my husband.

   B: What's _____ name?

4. A: I have one sister.

   B: What's _____ name?

C Complete the conversations.

1. A: Do you wash the dishes?

   B: Yes, _____ I do _____.

2. A: _____ you take out the garbage?

   B: No, I don't.

3. A: Do you do the laundry?

   B: Yes, I _____.

4. A: Do you _____ dinner?

   B: Yes, I do.

5. A: _____ you clean the house?

   B: No, I _____.

6. A: _____ you vacuum?

   B: Yes, I _____.

ROLE-PLAY.

Show pictures of your family. Or talk about this picture.

Student A
Ask about Student B's family.

Student B
Ask about Student A's family.

A: Who's that?

B: That's my _____.

A: What's _____ name?

B: _____.

LIFE SKILLS AND WRITING REVIEW

1 LIFE SKILLS: Fill out a form

Fill out the form.

Student Information Form

T L C
The Language Center

○ Mr. ○ Mrs. ○ Miss ○ Ms.

Name   **Today's Date**

First   Middle   Last

Date of Birth **Place of Birth** **Class**   **Teacher**

Class Schedule

Day/s   Time   Room

2 WRITE ABOUT YOURSELF

Complete the sentences.

1. My name is _____.
2. I'm from _____.
3. I'm in _____.
4. My teacher is _____.
5. I go to English class on _____.
6. Class starts at _____.

Unit Review: Go back to page 65. Which unit goals can you check off?

5 How Much Is It?

PREVIEW

Look at the picture. Who do you see?
What are they doing?

UNIT GOALS

☐ Make change with U.S. coins
☐ Make change with U.S. bills
☐ Ask where things are in a store
☐ Ask for and say prices
☐ Read and write about shopping

☐ **Life skills:** Read a receipt
☐ **English at work:** Answer a customer's questions

Make Change with U.S. Coins

Do you have change for a dollar?

1 VOCABULARY: U.S. coins

A Look at the pictures. What do you see?

▶ Listen and point. Listen and repeat.

1

2

3

4

5

B ▶ Listen and read. Listen and repeat.

1. a penny	**2.** a nickel	**3.** a dime
4. a quarter	**5.** a half-dollar	

C **MAKE CONNECTIONS.** Take out your coins. Count the coins. Tell your partner.

I have three quarters.

2 CONVERSATION

A ▶ Listen. Listen and repeat.

A: Excuse me. Do you have change for a dollar?

B: Yes. I have two quarters and five dimes. Here you go.

A: Thanks.

B Practice the conversation.

Make Change with U.S. Coins

C Look at the pictures. Complete the sentences.

1. A: Do you have change for a dollar?
   B: Yes. I have _____.

2. A: Do you have change for a dollar?
   B: Yes. I have _____.

3. A: Do you have change for a quarter?
   B: Yes. I have _____.

4. A: Do you have change for a quarter?
   B: Yes. I have _____.

D ▶ Listen and check your answers. Listen and repeat.

Show what you know!

1. WRITE ABOUT IT. Complete the conversation.

A: Do you have change for a _____?
B: Yes. I have _____. Here you go.
A: Thanks.

2. TELL THE CLASS. Role-play your conversation with a partner.

I can make change with U.S. coins. ■   I need more practice. ■

Make Change with U.S. Bills

Do you have change for a ten?

1 VOCABULARY: U.S. bills

Ⓐ Look at the pictures. What do you see?

▶ Listen and point. Listen and repeat.

1

2

3

4

5

6

Ⓑ ▶ Listen and read. Listen and repeat.

1. one dollar	**2.** five dollars
3. ten dollars	**4.** twenty dollars
5. fifty dollars	**6.** one hundred dollars

Ⓒ **WORK TOGETHER.** Say a bill. Your partner points to the picture.

Make Change with U.S. Bills

2 CONVERSATION

A ▶ **Listen. Listen and repeat.**

A: Excuse me. Do you have change for a ten?
B: Yes. I have a five and five ones. Here you go.
A: Great.

B **Practice the conversation.**

C **Look at the pictures. Complete the sentences.**

1. **A:** Do you have change for a five?
   B: Yes. I have _____.

2. **A:** Do you have change for a twenty?
   B: Yes. I have _____.

3. **A:** Do you have change for a fifty?
   B: Yes. I have _____.

4. **A:** Do you have change for a hundred?
   B: Yes. I have _____.

D ▶ **Listen and check your answers. Listen and repeat.**

Show what you know!

1. **WRITE ABOUT IT.** Complete the conversation.

   A: Excuse me. Do you have change for a _____?
   B: Yes. I have _____. Here you go.
   A: Great.

2. **TALK ABOUT IT.** Practice your conversation with a partner.

I can make change with U.S. bills. ■   I need more practice. □

Where is the soap?

1 VOCABULARY: Drugstore items

A Look at the pictures. What do you see?

▶ Listen and point. Listen and repeat.

B ▶ Listen and read. Listen and repeat.

1. soap	2. deodorant	3. toilet paper	4. paper towels
5. toothpaste	6. shaving cream	7. batteries	8. light bulbs
9. shampoo	10. aspirin	11. razors	12. tissues

C **WORK TOGETHER.** Point to a picture. Your partner says the word.

2 GRAMMAR: *Where is, where are*

Where is the soap?
Where is the aspirin?

Where are the razors?
Where are the tissues?

A Complete the sentences. Write *is* or *are*.

1. Where _____ *is* _____ the shampoo?
2. Where _____ the paper towels?
3. Where _____ the shaving cream?
4. Where _____ the light bulbs?
5. Where _____ the batteries?

B ▶ Listen and check your answers. Listen and repeat.

Show what you know!

1. **WRITE ABOUT IT.** Look at the signs. Write questions.

Where is the _____?

Where are the _____?

Aisle **1**
deodorant
shaving cream
razors

Aisle **2**
toothpaste
shampoo
soap

Aisle **3**
paper towels
toilet paper
tissues

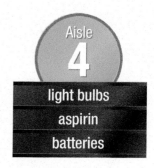

Aisle **4**
light bulbs
aspirin
batteries

2. **TALK ABOUT IT.** Ask and answer your questions.

A: Where is the soap?
B: Aisle 2.

I can ask where things are in a store. ■   I need more practice. ■

Ask for and Say Prices

How much is the toothpaste?

1 VOCABULARY: Prices

A ▶ Listen and point. Listen and repeat.

¢ = cents

15¢ 27¢ 49¢ 55¢ 75¢ 82¢ 99¢

B ▶ Listen. Write the prices.

1. _____ 2. _____ 3. _____

4. _____ 5. _____ 6. _____

C ▶ Listen and point. Listen and repeat.

$ = dollars

$1.50 $5.39 $10.25 $22.70 $36.00 $66.83 $93.99

D ▶ Listen. Write the prices.

1. _____ 2. _____ 3. _____

4. _____ 5. _____ 6. _____

7. _____ 8. _____ 9. _____

E WORK TOGETHER. Say a price. Your partner writes the price.

Ask for and Say Prices

2 CONVERSATION

A ▶ Listen. Listen and repeat.

A: Excuse me. How much is the toothpaste?
B: It's $3.99.
A: How much are the batteries?
B: They're $4.50.
A: Thanks.

B Practice the conversation.

C WORK TOGETHER. Look at the pictures. Make new conversations.

A: Excuse me. How much is the _____?
B: It's _____.
A: How much are the _____?
B: They're _____.
A: Thanks.

| $1.99 | $2.99 | $3.00 | $7.99 | $4.59 | $3.19 |

Show what you know!

1. **WRITE ABOUT IT.** Write a new price for each item.

   1. deodorant _____   **2.** soap _____
   3. shampoo _____   **4.** shaving cream _____
   5. aspirin _____   **6.** batteries _____

2. **TALK ABOUT IT.** Walk around the room. Ask about each item.
   How much is the deodorant?

I can ask for and say prices. ■   I need more practice. ■

Lesson 5

Swipe your card.

1 VOCABULARY

A Look at the pictures. What do you see?

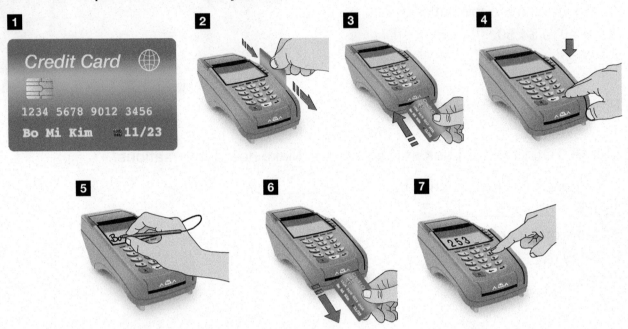

1 Credit Card
1234 5678 9012 3456
Bo Mi Kim 11/23

B ▶ Listen and read. Listen and repeat.

1. a card	**2.** swipe your card	**3.** insert your card	**4.** tap OK
5. sign your name	**6.** remove your card	**7.** enter your PIN	

C Write the words on the correct lines.

enter your PIN	insert	sign	swipe	tap

Life Skills: Read a Receipt

2 READING

A Read the receipt.

Family Drugstore

Date> 3/4/19

1 Shampoo	$5.79
1 Soap	2.99
1 Tissues	3.79
1 Razors	5.99
1 Shaving cream	6.25
1 Batteries	6.99

Transaction Total:

6 items

Subtotal	$31.80
Tax	2.23
Total	$34.03

Paid by: Credit card $34.03

B Circle *Yes* or *No*.

1. The name of the store is Drugstore.   Yes   No
2. The date on the receipt is March 4, 2019.   Yes   No
3. The person is buying five items.   Yes   No
4. The person is paying with a card.   Yes   No

3 WRITING

A Complete the sentences.

1. The shampoo is _____.
2. The tissues are _____.
3. The razors are _____.
4. The shaving cream is _____.
5. The tax is _____.
6. The total is _____.

B GO ONLINE.

1. Find an online drugstore.
2. Write the prices of items you want to buy. Add the prices. What is your total?

I can read a receipt. ■   I need more practice. ■

Read and Write About Shopping

This is Edna.

1 LISTENING

A Look at each picture. What do you see?

B ▶ Listen to the story.

Read and Write About Shopping

2 READING

A ▶ **Read and listen.**

This is Edna. In her native country, she shops at a market.
She talks about the price. She asks for a better price.
She is happy.
In the United States, Edna shops in a big store.
Each item has one price.
Edna pays a good price in the United States, too. She buys things on sale.

B Circle *Yes* or *No*.

1. Edna is from the United States.	Yes	No
2. In Edna's native country, she shops at a big store.	Yes	No
3. In Edna's native country, she asks for a better price.	Yes	No
4. In the United States, Edna shops at a big store.	Yes	No
5. In the United States, Edna buys things on sale.	Yes	No

3 WRITING

A **MAKE CONNECTIONS.** Talk about shopping in your native country.

1. Do people shop at markets? Do they shop in big stores?
2. Do people ask for a better price?
3. Do people pay good prices?

B Complete the sentences.

1. In my native country, people _____.
2. In the United States, people _____.
3. In _____, people pay a good price.
4. In _____, each item has one price.

C **WORK TOGETHER.** Read your sentences.

I can read and write about shopping. ■   I need more practice. ■

Fatima is at work.

1 READING

Fatima is a cashier.
She works in a store.
She makes change for a customer.

2 CONVERSATION AT WORK

A Complete the conversation. Write the correct words.

Customer:	_____. How much are	Excuse me	Great
	the batteries?		
Fatima:	Let me see. _____ $4.79.	It's	They're
Customer:	OK. I need new batteries.		
Fatima:	The total is $4.95.		
Customer:	_____ change for a ten?	Do you have	I have
Fatima:	Yes, I do.		
Customer:	Great. _____.	No, I don't	Here you go
Fatima:	Thank you. Here is your		
	_____.	change	total

B Practice the conversation.

C Role-play the conversation with new information.

I can answer a customer's questions. ■	I need more practice. ■

VOCABULARY REVIEW

A Write the name of the coin. Write the amount.

dime	nickel	quarter	5¢	25¢
half dollar	penny	1¢	10¢	50¢

_____ _____ _____ _____ _____

_____ _____ _____ _____ _____

B Point to a bill. Say the amount.

C WORK TOGETHER. Ask for change.

A: Excuse me. Do you have change for _____?

B: Yes. I have _____. Here you go.

A: Thanks.

GRAMMAR REVIEW

A Complete the sentences. Write *Where is* or *Where are*.

1. ___Where is___ the deodorant?
2. _____ the shaving cream?
3. _____ the tissues?
4. _____ the shampoo?
5. _____ the batteries?
6. _____ the razors?

B Complete the sentences. Write *How much is* or *How much are*.

1. ___How much is___ the aspirin?
2. _____ the toilet paper?
3. _____ the soap?
4. _____ the paper towels?
5. _____ the toothpaste?
6. _____ the light bulbs?

C Answer the questions from Exercise B.

1. The aspirin ___is $3.79.___ $3.79

2. The toilet paper _____ $3.49

3. The soap _____ $1.99

4. The paper towels _____ $4.99

5. The toothpaste _____ $5.79

6. The light bulbs _____ $3.99

ROLE-PLAY.

Student A
Look at the pictures.
Ask Student B where something is.

Student B
Answer Student A's question.

A: Excuse me. Where _____ the _____?

B: Aisle _____.

A: Thanks.

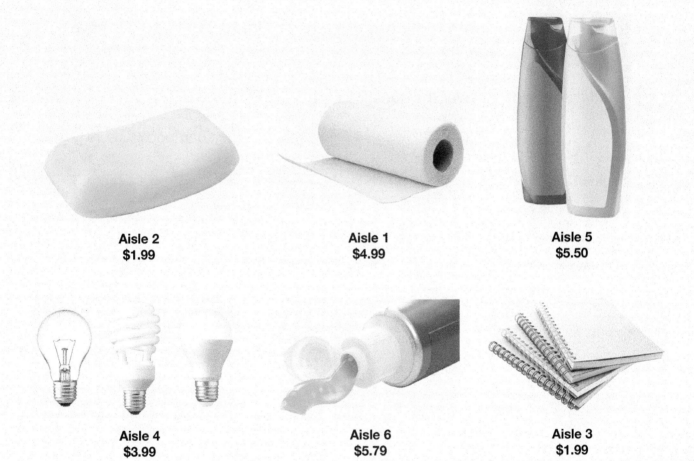

Aisle 2
$1.99

Aisle 1
$4.99

Aisle 5
$5.50

Aisle 4
$3.99

Aisle 6
$5.79

Aisle 3
$1.99

Student B
Look at the pictures.
Ask Student A how much something is.

Student A
Answer Student B's question.

B: Excuse me. How much _____ the _____?

A: It's _____. (They're _____.)

B: Thanks.

LIFE SKILLS AND WRITING REVIEW

1 LIFE SKILLS: Read a receipt

A Circle the correct word.

1. Swipe your _____.		card	PIN
2. _____ your card.		Tap	Insert
3. _____ OK.		Tap	Sign
4. _____ your name.		Sign	Insert
5. Enter your _____.		PIN	card
6. _____ your card.		Tap	Remove
7. _____ with a card.		Pay	Sign

B Read the receipt. Answer the questions.

CDS Drugstore

Date> 8/11/19

1 Shampoo	$4.79
1 Soap	1.89
1 Tissues	3.99
1 Razors	5.50
1 Paper towels	4.25

Transaction Total:

5 items	Subtotal	$20.42
	Tax	1.43
	Total	$21.85

Paid by: Credit card $21.85

1. How much is the shampoo?

_____

2. How much are the paper towels?

_____

3. What is the date on the receipt?

_____

4. How much is the total?

_____

2 WRITE ABOUT YOURSELF

Complete the sentences.

1. My name is _____.

2. I shop at _____.

3. I buy _____.

4. I pay with _____.

Unit Review: Go back to page 85. Which unit goals can you check off?

6 Let's Eat

PREVIEW

Look at the picture. Who do you see?
Where are they?

LEMON 99¢ EACH

100% ORGANIC

UNIT GOALS

- ☐ Talk about vegetables
- ☐ Say what you like and don't like
- ☐ Say what someone likes and doesn't like
- ☐ Ask what someone needs

- ☐ Read a menu and order food
- ☐ Read and write about eating
- ☐ **Life skills:** Read an ad; Make a shopping list
- ☐ **English at work:** Do an inventory

Talk About Vegetables

Do we need vegetables?

1 VOCABULARY: Vegetables

A Look at the pictures. What do you see?

▶ Listen and point. Listen and repeat.

B ▶ Listen and read. Listen and repeat.

1. tomatoes	**2.** carrots	**3.** cucumbers
4. onions	**5.** peppers	**6.** lettuce
7. potatoes	**8.** mushrooms	**9.** peas

C **WORK TOGETHER.** Point to a picture. Your partner says the word.

Talk About Vegetables

2 CONVERSATION

A ▶ Listen. Listen and repeat.

A: Hi. I'm at the store. Do we need vegetables?
B: Yes. We need tomatoes and carrots.
A: OK. Do we need onions?
B: No. We have onions.

B Practice the conversation.

C WORK TOGETHER. Make new conversations.

A: Hi. I'm at the store. Do we need vegetables?
B: Yes. We need _____ and _____.
A: OK. Do we need _____?
B: No. We have _____.

D ▶ Listen and read.

Pam

Hi, I'm Pam. It's time to make vegetable soup!
I have tomatoes, onions, peas, and potatoes.
I need mushrooms and carrots.

E Circle *Yes* or *No*.

1. Pam has mushrooms.	Yes	No
2. She needs tomatoes.	Yes	No
3. She has onions.	Yes	No
4. She needs carrots.	Yes	No

Show what you know!

1. **WRITE ABOUT IT.** What vegetables do you have at home?

   I have _____.

2. **TALK ABOUT IT.** Tell your partner.

   I have peas and carrots.

I can talk about vegetables. ■   I need more practice. ■

Lesson 2

Do you like vegetables?

1 CONVERSATION

A ▶ **Listen. Listen and repeat.**

A: Do you like vegetables?
B: I like tomatoes. I don't like onions.
   What about you?
A: I like peppers. I don't like carrots.

B ▶ **Listen again. Check (✓) the vegetables they like.**

☐ tomatoes
☐ onions
☐ peppers
☐ carrots

C ▶ **Listen again. Check (✓) the vegetables they don't like.**

☐ tomatoes
☐ onions
☐ peppers
☐ carrots

D Practice the conversation.

E **WORK TOGETHER.** Make new conversations.

A: Do you like vegetables?
B: I like _____.
   I don't like _____. What about you?
A: I like _____.
   I don't like _____.

Say What You Like and Don't Like

2 GRAMMAR: *Like, don't like*

I **like** tomatoes.	I **don't like** onions. I **do not like** onions.
You **like** lettuce.	You **don't like** carrots. You **do not like** carrots.
Luz and Pavel **like** potatoes.	They **don't like** peas. They **do not like** peas.
John and I **like** cucumbers.	We **don't like** mushrooms. We **do not like** mushrooms.

Complete the sentences. Use *like* and *don't like*.

do not = don't

1. I _like cucumbers_____.

2. Carlos and Susan _____.

3. We _____.

4. You _____.

5. I _____.

Show what you know!

1. WRITE ABOUT IT. Write about food you like and don't like.

I like _____, _____, and _____.

I don't like _____, _____, or _____.

I can say what I like and don't like. ■   I need more practice. ■

Say What Someone Likes and Doesn't Like

Does your daughter like fruit?

1 VOCABULARY: Fruit

A Look at the pictures. What do you see?

▶ Listen and point. Listen and repeat.

B ▶ Listen and read. Listen and repeat.

1. apples	**2.** cherries	**3.** mangoes
4. oranges	**5.** pears	**6.** strawberries
7. bananas	**8.** peaches	**9.** grapes

C Write three fruits you like.

_____   _____   _____

D WORK TOGETHER. Tell your partner.

I like _____.

Say What Someone Likes and Doesn't Like

2 CONVERSATION

A ▶ **Listen. Listen and repeat.**

A: Does your daughter like fruit?
B: She likes apples. She doesn't like pears.

B **Practice the conversation.**

3 GRAMMAR: *Likes, doesn't like*

My daughter **likes** apples.	She **doesn't like** pears. She **does not like** pears.
My son **likes** oranges.	He **doesn't like** bananas. He **does not like** bananas.
Tara **likes** pears.	She **doesn't like** mangoes. She **does not like** mangoes.

> does not = doesn't

Complete the sentences.

1. My mother ___*likes*___ grapes.
              like

2. My teacher _____ peaches.
                    not / like

3. He _____ apples.
         not / like

4. She _____ bananas.
          like

Show what you know!

1. TALK ABOUT IT. Talk to your classmates. Complete the chart.

I like _____. I don't like _____.

Name	Likes	Doesn't Like

2. WRITE ABOUT IT. Write sentences.

Olga likes apples. She doesn't like pears.

I can say what someone likes and doesn't like. ☐	I need more practice. ☐

Ask What Someone Needs

Do you need anything from the store?

1 VOCABULARY: Amounts

▶ Listen and point. Listen and repeat.

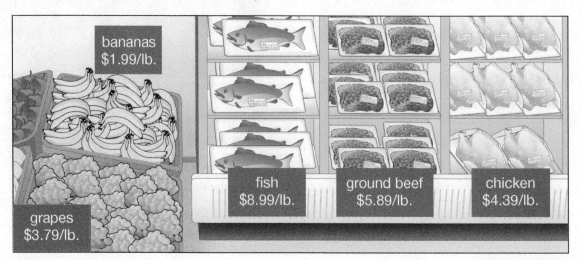

bananas $1.99/lb.

grapes $3.79/lb.

fish $8.99/lb.

ground beef $5.89/lb.

chicken $4.39/lb.

lb. = pound
lbs. = pounds

2 CONVERSATION

A ▶ Listen. Listen and repeat.

A: Do you need anything from the store?
B: Yes. I need one pound of grapes and two pounds of ground beef.

B Practice the conversation.

C WORK TOGETHER. Look at the shopping lists. Make new conversations.

A: Do you need anything from the store?
B: Yes. I need _____ and _____.

Shopping List 1	Shopping List 2	Shopping List 3
2 lbs. of grapes	1 lb. of fish	3 lbs. of bananas
1 lb. of bananas	2 lbs. of ground beef	4 lbs. of chicken

Ask What Someone Needs

3 VOCABULARY: Containers

▶ Listen and point. Listen and repeat.

a gallon of milk

a loaf of bread

a box of cereal

a dozen eggs   **a bag of rice**   **a can of soup**

Singular		Plural
bag	→	bags
box	→	boxes
can	→	cans
dozen	→	two dozen
gallon	→	gallons
loaf	→	loaves

4 CONVERSATION

A ▶ Listen. Listen and repeat.

A: What do we need from the store?
B: We need a bag of rice and two dozen eggs.

B Practice the conversation.

C WORK TOGETHER. Look at the pictures. Make new conversations.

A: What do we need from the store?
B: We need _____ and _____.

Conversation 1

Conversation 2

Conversation 3

Show what you know!

1. TALK ABOUT IT. What do you need from the store?

I need _____.

2. WRITE ABOUT IT. Write sentences.

Ann needs a pound of grapes.

I can ask what someone needs. ■	I need more practice. ■

Lesson 5

How much is bread?

1 READING

A ▶ Listen and read.

Shop Mart Weekly Specials

Loaf of bread
$1.79

One dozen eggs
$1.29

Chicken
$1.99/lb.

Tomato soup
79¢
Buy one, get one free

Cereal
$4.25

Bananas 49¢/lb.

B Circle the answer.

1. How much is bread?
   $1.79 a loaf $1.79 a pound

2. How much is one dozen eggs?
   99¢ $1.29

3. How much is chicken?
   $1.99 each $1.99 a pound

4. How much is a can of tomato soup?
   $1.79   79¢

5. How much is cereal?
   $4.25 a box $4.25 a pound

6. How much are two pounds of bananas?
   98¢ $1.49

2 WRITING

A Look at the pictures. Write the shopping lists.

2 dozen eggs
1 pound of chicken
2 cans of soup

B WORK TOGETHER. Read your lists to your classmate.

C GO ONLINE.

1. Find food prices on your favorite supermarket's website or app.
2. Write the foods you need and the prices you see.

Food	Price
_____	_____
_____	_____
_____	_____

I can read an ad. ■   I need more practice. ■

6

Are you ready to order?

1 VOCABULARY: Food on a menu

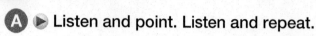 Listen and point. Listen and repeat.

a tuna fish sandwich   a chicken sandwich   a cheeseburger   a baked potato

a green salad   a fruit salad   French fries   rice

pancakes   eggs and toast   cereal

iced tea   juice   coffee   tea

B WORK TOGETHER. Say a food. Your partner points to the picture.

Read a Menu and Order Food

2 CONVERSATION

A ▶ Listen. Listen and repeat.

A: Are you ready to order?

B: Yes. I'd like a tuna fish sandwich, a green salad, and an iced tea.

A: Anything else?

B: No, thank you.

B Practice the conversation.

Show what you know!

1. WRITE ABOUT IT. Look at the menu. Write foods you'd like.

I'd like _____, _____, and _____.

Breakfast		French fries	$3.75
pancakes	$4.50	baked potato	$2.50
eggs and toast	$4.00	rice	$2.25
cereal	$3.00	green salad	$3.50
		fruit salad	$4.00
Lunch and Dinner			
cheeseburger	$4.50	**Drinks**	
chicken sandwich	$4.00	juice	$3.00
tuna fish sandwich	$5.00	coffee	$2.25
		tea	$2.25
		iced tea	$2.00

2. TELL THE CLASS. Order food from the menu.

I'd like a cheeseburger, a fruit salad, and juice.

I can read a menu and order food. ■   I need more practice. ■

Read and Write About Eating

This is Tran.

A Look at each picture. What do you see?

B ▶ Listen to the story.

Read and Write About Eating

2 READING

A ▶ **Read and listen.**

This is Tran. In his native country, most people eat with chopsticks.
Many children eat with their hands.
This is Riko. In her native country, many people drink soup.
In the United States, most people eat with a fork, knife, and spoon.
They eat sandwiches and French fries with their hands.

B Circle *Yes* or *No*.

1. Tran eats with chopsticks.	Yes	No
2. In Tran's native country, many children eat with their hands.	Yes	No
3. In Riko's native country, people eat soup with a spoon.	Yes	No
4. In the United States, most people use a knife and fork.	Yes	No
5. In the United States, people eat sandwiches with chopsticks.	Yes	No

3 WRITING

A **MAKE CONNECTIONS.** Talk about eating in your native country.

1. Do people eat with chopsticks?

2. Do people eat with their hands?

3. Do people eat with a knife, fork, and spoon?

B Complete the sentences.

1. In my native country, most people eat with _____.

2. Children eat with _____.

3. In the United States, most people eat with _____.

C **WORK TOGETHER.** Read your sentences.

I can read and write about eating. ■   I need more practice. ■

English at Work: Do an Inventory

Sara is at work.

Sara

Carlos

1 | READING

Sara is a cook.
She works in a restaurant.
She does an inventory with Carlos.

2 | CONVERSATION AT WORK

A Complete the conversation. Write the correct words.

Carlos: _____ ground beef?

Sara: Yes, we need _____ of ground beef.

Do you like	Do we need
four gallons	four pounds

Carlos: OK, got it. What about vegetables? What do we need?

Sara: Let's see. _____ carrots, potatoes, and lettuce.

We need	She needs

Carlos: Anything else?

Sara: Oh! We need three _____ of milk.

gallons	loaves

B Practice the conversation.

C Role-play the conversation with new information.

I can do an inventory. ■	I need more practice. ■

VOCABULARY REVIEW

A Look at the picture. Write the foods.

B Circle the word that does not belong in each group.

1. apples	cucumbers	pears
2. lettuce	carrots	oranges
3. chicken	ground beef	lemons
4. rice	bread	apples
5. mushrooms	milk	onions
6. cherries	eggs	grapes
7. cereal	potatoes	tomatoes
8. peas	mangoes	strawberries

C WORK TOGETHER. Write one word for each quantity.

1. a pound of _____

2. a bag of _____

3. a box of _____

4. a loaf of _____

5. a dozen _____

GRAMMAR REVIEW

A Complete the sentences. Write *like* or *likes*.

1. I _____like_____ carrots.
2. Tara _____ peas.
3. Tom and Sue _____ apples.
4. We _____ bread.
5. Jim _____ milk.
6. They _____ vegetable soup.
7. Kara _____ pancakes.

B Complete the sentences. Write *don't like* or *doesn't like*.

1. Bob and Tran ____don't like____ juice.
2. I _____ onions.
3. Kate _____ eggs.
4. We _____ bananas.
5. Jack _____ eggs.
6. They _____ grapes.
7. She _____ bread.

C Complete the conversations. Write *I like* or *I'd like*.

1. **A:** Do you like fruit?
   B: Yes. _____I like_____ apples.
2. **A:** Are you ready to order?
   B: Yes. _____ pancakes.
3. **A:** Do you like vegetables?
   B: _____ peas.
4. **A:** Are you ready to order?
   B: _____ a cheeseburger, please.

CONVERSATION REVIEW

ROLE-PLAY.

Student A
You are a server.
Ask for the customer's lunch order.
Write the order.

Student B
You are the customer.
Look at the menu.
Order lunch.

Breakfast		French fries	$3.75
pancakes	$4.50	baked potato	$2.50
eggs and toast	$4.00	rice	$2.25
cereal	$3.00	green salad	$3.50
		fruit salad	$4.00
Lunch and Dinner			
cheeseburger	$4.50	**Drinks**	
chicken sandwich	$4.00	juice	$3.00
tuna fish sandwich	$5.00	coffee	$2.25
		tea	$2.25
		iced tea	$2.00

A: Are you ready to order?

B: Yes. I'd like _____, _____, and _____.

A: Anything else?

B: _____.

Switch roles.

B: Are you ready to order?

A: Yes. I'd like _____, _____, and _____.

B: Anything else?

A: _____.

1 LIFE SKILLS: Make a shopping list

A ▶ Listen. Complete the shopping list.

_____ of rice

_____ eggs

a pound of _____

_____ of chicken

B MAKE CONNECTIONS. What do you need? Write a shopping list.

2 WRITE ABOUT YOURSELF

Complete the sentences.

1. I shop for fruits and vegetables at _____.
2. I shop for bread at _____.
3. I shop for meat at _____.
4. I also buy _____.
5. My favorite restaurant is _____.
   I like _____ there.

Unit Review: Go back to page 103. Which unit goals can you check off?

7 Apartment for Rent

PREVIEW

Look at the picture. Who do you see?
Where are they?

UNIT GOALS

- [ ] Identify rooms in a home
- [ ] Talk about a home
- [ ] Ask about furniture and appliances
- [ ] Give an address
- [ ] Read and write about moving
- [ ] **Life skills:** Address an envelope
- [ ] **English at work:** Talk about apartments

Identify Rooms in a Home

I have a new apartment.

1 VOCABULARY: Rooms in a home

A Look at the picture. What do you see?

▶ Listen and point. Listen and repeat.

B ▶ Listen and read. Listen and repeat.

1. bedroom	**2.** bathroom	**3.** closet
4. living room	**5.** dining room	**6.** kitchen
7. laundry room	**8.** basement	**9.** garage

C **WORK TOGETHER.** Point to a room. Your partner names it.

Identify Rooms in a Home

2 CONVERSATION

A ▶ Listen. Listen and repeat.

A: Guess what? I have a new apartment.
B: Really? What's it like?
A: It has a kitchen, a living room, and one bedroom.
B: It sounds great!

B Practice the conversation.

C WORK TOGETHER. Look at the pictures. Make new conversations.

A: Guess what? I have a new apartment.
B: Really? What's it like?
A: It has _____.
B: It sounds great!

Conversation 1

Conversation 2

Show what you know!

1. **WRITE ABOUT IT.** Write the rooms in your home.

   My home has _____, _____, and _____.

2. **TELL THE CLASS.** Talk about the rooms in your home.

   My home has a kitchen, two bedrooms, and one bathroom.

I can identify rooms in a home. ☐   I need more practice. ☐

Can you tell me about the apartment?

1 VOCABULARY: Words to describe rooms

▶ Listen and point. Listen and repeat.

sunny   new   large   small

2 CONVERSATION

A ▶ Listen. Listen and repeat.

A: Can you tell me about the apartment for rent?
B: There is a sunny bedroom, a new kitchen, and a large living room.
A: It sounds nice.

B Practice the conversation.

C WORK TOGETHER. Look at the apartments. Make new conversations.

A: Can you tell me about the apartment for rent?
B: There is a _____, a _____, and a _____.
A: It sounds nice.

Conversation 1

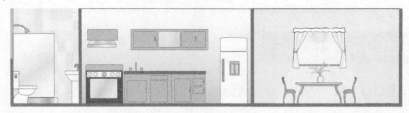

Conversation 2

Talk About a Home

3 GRAMMAR: *There is, there are*

There is a kitchen.
There is a living room.

There are two bedrooms.
There are two bathrooms.

A Complete the sentences. Write *There is* or *There are*.

I like my home. _____There are_____ six rooms. _____ two

small bedrooms. _____ a living room. _____

a new kitchen. _____ a large bathroom. _____

a laundry room in the basement.

B Circle *Yes* or *No*.

1. There are three rooms.   Yes   No
2. The bedrooms are small.   Yes   No
3. The kitchen is old.   Yes   No
4. There is a laundry room.   Yes   No

Show what you know!

1. **WRITE ABOUT IT.** Write about your home.

   There is _____.
   There are _____.

2. **TALK ABOUT IT.** Talk about your home.

   There is a sunny living room.
   There are two small bedrooms.

Ask About Furniture and Appliances

Is there a refrigerator?

1 VOCABULARY: Furniture and appliances

Ⓐ Look at the pictures. What do you see?

▶ Listen and point. Listen and repeat.

Ⓑ ▶ Listen and read. Listen and repeat.

1. sink	**2.** dishwasher	**3.** stove	**4.** refrigerator
5. toilet	**6.** shower	**7.** bed	**8.** dresser
9. lamp	**10.** sofa	**11.** chair	**12.** table
13. washing machine	**14.** dryer		

Ⓒ What is in your home?

_____ _____ _____

_____ _____ _____

Ⓓ **MAKE CONNECTIONS.** Tell your classmate what is in your home.

Ask About Furniture and Appliances

2 CONVERSATION

A ▶ Listen. Listen and repeat.

A: I have some questions about the apartment. Is there a refrigerator?

B: Yes, there is.

A: Are there any lamps?

B: No, there aren't.

B Practice the conversation.

3 GRAMMAR: *Is there, are there*

Is there a dishwasher?	Yes, **there is.**	No, **there isn't.** No, **there's not.**
Are there any beds?	Yes, **there are.**	No, **there aren't.** No, **there are not.**

A Complete the questions and the answers.

there is = there's
is not = isn't
are not = aren't

1. **A:** _____Is there_____ a stove?
   B: Yes, _____.

2. **A:** _____ any chairs?
   B: Yes, _____.

3. **A:** _____ any lamps?
   B: No, _____.

4. **A:** _____ a washing machine?
   B: No, _____.

B ▶ Listen and check your answers. Listen and repeat.

Show what you know!

1. TALK ABOUT IT. Ask about your partner's home.

Is there a _____?
Are there any _____?

2. WRITE ABOUT IT. Write about your partner's home.

There is a washing machine.
There aren't any dressers.

I can ask about furniture and appliances. ■   I need more practice. ■

Give an Address

What's the address?

1 VOCABULARY: Addresses

A ▶ Listen and point. Listen and repeat.

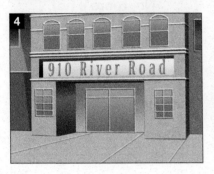

B ▶ Listen. Circle the address.

1.	207 John Lane	270 John Lane
2.	15 City Street	51 City Street
3.	1460 Third Avenue	1640 Third Avenue
4.	40 Park Drive	60 Park Drive
5.	309 Sun Boulevard	319 Sun Boulevard

C ▶ Listen. Complete the addresses.

1. _____ Sandy Boulevard
2. _____ West Avenue
3. _____ Main Street
4. _____ Jones Road
5. _____ North Drive
6. _____ Town Lane

Give an Address

2 CONVERSATION

A ▶ Listen. Listen and repeat.

A: I'm looking for an apartment.
B: Oh! There's an apartment for rent on my street.
A: What's the address?
B: It's 1630 River Street.
A: How much is the rent?
B: It's $900 a month.

B Circle *Yes* or *No*.

1. There is an apartment for rent on her street.   Yes   No
2. The address is 1260 River Street.   Yes   No
3. The rent is $900 a month.   Yes   No

C Practice the conversation.

Show what you know!

1. TALK ABOUT IT. Read the ads. Make new conversations.

Conversation 1	**Conversation 2**	**Conversation 3**
● ● ●	● ● ●	● ● ●
1 bedroom	3 bedrooms	2 bedrooms
658 River Drive	1920 Park Lane	19 Bank Street
$975/month	$1,300/month	$1,125/month

A: I'm looking for an apartment.
B: Oh! There's an apartment for rent on my street.
A: What's the address?
B: It's _____.
A: How much is the rent?
B: It's _____.

2. WRITE ABOUT IT. Write one of your conversations.

I can give an address. ■   I need more practice. ■

Life Skills: Address an Envelope

Who is the letter from?

1 VOCABULARY

Write the abbreviation.

Apt.	Ave.	Blvd.	Dr.	Ln.	Rd.	St.

1. Street _____
2. Avenue _____
3. Drive _____
4. Lane _____
5. Road _____
6. Boulevard _____
7. Apartment _____

2 READING

A Read the envelope.

return address —— Dave Clark
9106 River Rd. Apt. 115
Chicago, IL 60623

street address ———————— Tina Smith
7754 Park Ave.
Chicago, IL 60647

city ———

state ———

ZIP code ———

B Circle the answers.

1. Who is the letter from?
2. What is the return address?
3. Who is the letter to?
4. What is Tina's ZIP code?
5. What is Dave's ZIP code?

Tina Smith	Dave Clark
9106 River Rd.	7754 Park Ave.
Tina Smith	Dave Clark
60647	60326
60623	60547

Life Skills: Address an Envelope

3 WRITING

A Answer the questions.

1. What's your first and last name? _____
2. What's your street address? _____
3. What's your city and state? _____
4. What's your ZIP code? _____

B GO ONLINE.

1. Find a business online. Find the business's address. Answer the questions.

   a. What's the name of the business?

   _____

   b. What's the street address?

   _____

   c. What's the city and state?

   _____

   d. What's the ZIP code?

   _____

2. Address an envelope to the business. Write your address for the return address.

| I can address an envelope. ■ | I need more practice. ■ |

This is Pilar.

1 LISTENING

A Look at each picture. What do you see?

B ▶ Listen to the story.

Read and Write About Moving

2 READING

A ► Read and listen.

This is Pilar. She is 21 years old. She is single.

Pilar lives with her sister and her sister's husband.

Pilar has a good job. She works in an office.

Pilar wants to live with her friends. In the United States, many single people live with friends.

Pilar's parents are not happy. In their native country, single people live with their families.

B Circle *Yes* or *No*.

1. Pilar lives with her parents.	Yes	No
2. Pilar has a job.	Yes	No
3. Pilar wants to live with her friends.	Yes	No
4. Pilar's parents want Pilar to live with her friends.	Yes	No
5. In the United States, many single people live with friends.	Yes	No

3 WRITING

A MAKE CONNECTIONS. Talk about where people live in your native country.

1. Do single people live with their families?
2. Do single people live with friends?

B Complete the sentences.

1. In my native country, many single people live _____.
2. In the United States, many single people live _____.

C WORK TOGETHER. Read your sentences.

I can read and write about moving. ■   I need more practice. ■

Vera is at work.

1 READING

Vera is a building manager.
She works in an apartment building.
She helps people rent apartments.

2 CONVERSATION AT WORK

A Complete the conversation. Write the correct words.

Vera:	Good morning. Can I help you?
Customer:	Good morning. I'm looking for a two-bedroom apartment.
Vera:	OK. I have an apartment _____ on River Street.
Customer:	What's it like?
Vera:	_____ two bedrooms, a kitchen, and a living room.
Customer:	It sounds great! _____?
Vera:	It's $1,150 a month.
Customer:	What's the _____?
Vera:	It's 32 River Street.

for sale   for rent

There is   There are

How much   What's the
is the rent   address

kitchen   address

B Practice the conversation.

C Role-play the conversation with new information.

I can talk about apartments. ■   I need more practice. ■

VOCABULARY REVIEW

A ▶ **LISTEN.** Listen and repeat.

bathroom	bed	bedroom	chair	dining room
dryer	kitchen	lamp	living room	refrigerator
sink	sofa	stove	table	washing machine

B Look at Exercise A. Circle the furniture and appliances. Underline the rooms.

C Look at the picture. Write the words.

1. _____

2. _____

3. _____

4. _____

GRAMMAR REVIEW

A Complete the sentences. Write *There is* or *There are*.

I have a great apartment. _____*There is*_____ a large living room. _____
two sunny bedrooms. _____ a new kitchen. _____ a table in
the kitchen. _____ four chairs. _____ a laundry room in the
basement. _____ a bathroom. _____ a shower in the bathroom.
_____ two sinks.

B Complete the conversations.

1. A: _____*Is there*_____ a laundry room?

    B: No, _____.

2. A: _____ any dressers?

    B: Yes, _____.

3. A: _____ any chairs?

    B: No, _____.

4. A: _____ a washing machine?

    B: No, _____.

5. A: _____ a dishwasher?

    B: Yes, _____.

6. A: _____ a garage?

    B: No, _____.

7. A: _____ any closets?

    B: Yes, _____.

8. A: _____ any beds?

    B: No, _____.

ROLE-PLAY.

Student A
There is an apartment with furniture for rent.
Ask about the apartment. Ask about:

the address	a refrigerator
the rent	chairs
a stove	a sunny living room

Student B
Look at the apartment.
Answer Student A's questions.

A: Can you tell me about the apartment? What's the address?

B: It's _____.

A: How much is the rent?

B: It's _____ a month.

A: Is there _____?

B: _____.

A: Are there any _____?

B: _____.

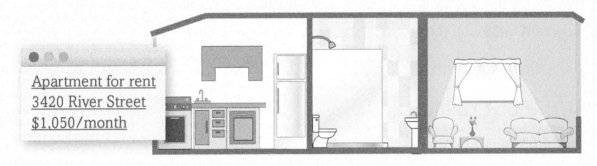

Apartment for rent
3420 River Street
$1,050/month

Student B
There is an apartment with furniture for rent.
Ask about the apartment. Ask about:

the address	a large bathroom
the rent	two bedrooms
a sofa	lamps

Student A
Look at the apartment.
Answer Student B's questions.

B: Can you tell me about the apartment? What's the address?

A: It's _____.

B: How much is the rent?

A: It's _____ a month.

B: Is there _____?

A: _____.

B: Are there any _____?

A: _____.

LIFE SKILLS AND WRITING REVIEW

1 LIFE SKILLS: Read an ad

A Read the ads.

FOR RENT 1 bedroom apartment New stove, refrigerator Living room has sofa and chairs $995/month Call Robert 613-555-8714	**FOR RENT** Apartment in house 2 bedrooms Garage Laundry room in basement $1,200/month Call Rosa 312-555-9312
A	**B**

B Read the sentences. Match the sentences with the ads. Write *A* or *B*.

1. There is furniture. _____
2. There are two bedrooms. _____
3. There is a new stove. _____
4. There is a laundry room. _____
5. The rent is $995 a month. _____
6. There is a garage. _____

2 WRITE ABOUT YOURSELF

Complete the sentences.

1. My favorite room is _____.
2. There is _____.
3. There are _____.

Unit Review: Go back to page 123. Which unit goals can you check off?

8 Let's Go Shopping

PREVIEW
Look at the picture. Who do you see?
What is he doing?

ALE
0% OFF

UNIT GOALS

☐ Identify clothing you need
☐ Ask for clothing sizes
☐ Describe clothing
☐ Return clothing to a store

☐ Read and write about clothing at a wedding
☐ **Life skills:** Read store ads
☐ **English at work:** Help a customer return clothes

Identify Clothing You Need

I need a new jacket.

1 VOCABULARY: Clothing

A Look at the pictures. What do you see?

▶ Listen and point. Listen and repeat.

B ▶ Listen and read. Listen and repeat.

1. a T-shirt	**2.** a skirt	**3.** a dress	**4.** a jacket
5. a shirt	**6.** a sweater	**7.** jeans	**8.** pants
9. socks	**10.** shoes	**11.** sneakers	

C MAKE CONNECTIONS. Look at your classmates. What clothing do you see?

Identify Clothing You Need

2 CONVERSATION

A ▶ Listen. Listen and repeat.

A: Let's go shopping! I need a new jacket.
B: OK. I need new shoes.

B Practice the conversation.

C **WORK TOGETHER.** Look at the pictures. Make new conversations.

A: Let's go shopping! I need a new _____.
B: OK. I need new _____.

Conversation 1

Conversation 2

Conversation 3

Show what you know!

1. WRITE ABOUT IT. What clothing do you need?

I need a new _____.
I need new _____.

2. TALK ABOUT IT. What clothing do you need?

I need a new dress.
I need new shoes.

| I can identify clothing I need. ■ | I need more practice. ■ |

Ask for Clothing Sizes

Do you have this shirt in large?

1 VOCABULARY: Clothing sizes

▶ Listen and point. Listen and repeat.

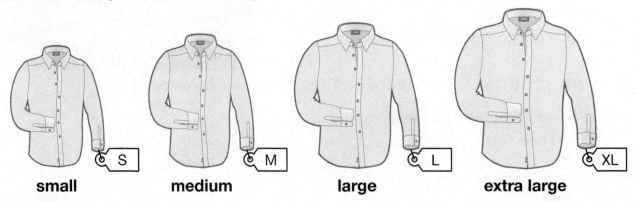

| small | medium | large | extra large |

2 CONVERSATION

A ▶ Listen. Listen and repeat.

A: Can I help you?
B: Do you have this shirt in large?
A: Yes. Here you go.
B: Do you have these pants in size 12?
A: No, I'm sorry. We don't.

B Practice the conversation.

C WORK TOGETHER. Look at the pictures. Make new conversations.

A: Can I help you?
B: Do you have this _____ in large?
A: Yes. Here you go.
B: Do you have these _____ in size 12?
A: No, I'm sorry. We don't.

| Conversation 1 | Conversation 2 | Conversation 3 |

Ask for Clothing Sizes

3 GRAMMAR: *This, that, these, those*

Do you have **this** shirt in large?

No, but we have **that** shirt in large.

Do you have **these** shirts in small?

No, but we have **those** shirts in small.

A Complete the sentences. Write *this* or *these*.

1. Do you have _____*this*_____ jacket in extra large?

2. Do you have _____ shoes in size 8?

3. We have _____ sweaters in small.

4. We have _____ dress in size 10.

5. We have _____ shirt in medium.

B Complete the sentences. Write *that* or *those*.

1. Do you have _____*those*_____ socks in a small?

2. Do you have _____ skirt in large?

3. We have _____ pants in size 16.

4. We have _____ T-shirts in extra large.

5. We have _____ shirt in size 6.

Show what you know!

1. WRITE ABOUT IT. Make a new conversation.

A: Do you have this _____ in _____?

B: No, I'm sorry. We don't. We have that _____ in _____.

A: Do you have these _____ in _____?

B: No, I'm sorry. We don't. We have those _____ in _____.

2. TALK ABOUT IT. Practice your conversation.

I can ask for clothing sizes. ☐   I need more practice. ☐

Describe Clothing

What does she have on?

A ▶ Listen and point. Listen and repeat.

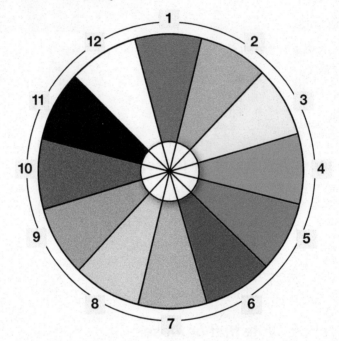

B ▶ Listen and read. Listen and repeat.

1. red	**2.** orange	**3.** yellow	**4.** green
5. blue	**6.** purple	**7.** pink	**8.** beige
9. gray	**10.** brown	**11.** black	**12.** white

C Write your answers.

1. What color is your favorite jacket?
My favorite jacket is _____.

2. What color are your favorite pants?
My favorite pants are _____.

3. What color are your favorite shoes?
My favorite shoes are _____.

4. What color is your favorite T-shirt?
My favorite T-shirt is _____.

5. What is your favorite color?
My favorite color is _____.

D WORK TOGETHER. Ask your classmate the questions in Exercise C.

Describe Clothing

2 CONVERSATION

A ▶ Listen. Listen and repeat.

A: Is Nina here?

B: Yes. She's over there.

A: Where? What does she have on?

B: She has on a red shirt and black pants.

A: OK. Thanks.

B Practice the conversation.

3 GRAMMAR: Adjective + noun

He has on a **white shirt.**
She has on a **red shirt** and **black pants.**

| Rob | Tina | Ling | Ed |

Complete the sentences.

1. Rob has on _gray pants and a white shirt_____.

2. Tina has on _____.

3. Ling has on _____.

4. Ed has on _____.

Show what you know!

1. **WRITE ABOUT IT.** Look at a classmate. What clothing does your classmate have on?

   My classmate has on _____ and _____.

2. **TELL THE CLASS.** Read your sentence to the class. Ask: *Who is it?*

I can describe clothing. ☐   I need more practice. ☐

What's the problem?

1 VOCABULARY: Problems with clothing

A ▶ Listen and point. Listen and repeat.

It's too small.

It's too big.

B ▶ Listen. Circle the problem.

1. too small   too big
2. too small   too big
3. too small   too big
4. too small   too big

2 CONVERSATION

A ▶ Listen. Listen and repeat.

A: I need to return this jacket and these shoes.
B: What's the problem?
A: The jacket is too big. The shoes are too small.
   Here's my receipt.

B Circle *Yes* or *No*.

1. The man is buying a jacket and shoes.   Yes   No
2. The jacket is too small.   Yes   No
3. The shoes are too small.   Yes   No
4. He has a receipt.   Yes   No

C Practice the conversation.

Return Clothing to a Store

D **WORK TOGETHER.** Look at the pictures. Make new conversations.

A: I need to return this _____ and these _____.

B: What's the problem?

A: The _____ is too _____. The _____ are too _____. Here's my receipt.

Conversation 1

Conversation 2

Show what you know!

1. TALK ABOUT IT. Talk about the pictures.

A: What's the problem?
B: The skirt is too _____.

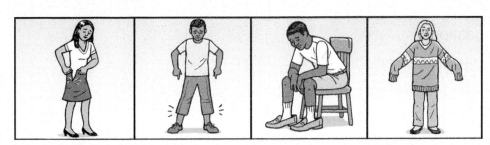

2. WRITE ABOUT IT. Write sentences about the pictures.

The skirt is too small.

I can return clothing to a store. ☐   I need more practice. ☐

Life Skills: Read Store Ads

Are shoes on sale?

1 READING

A Read the store ad.

CLOTHING MART Sale April 22-29 HOME | WOMEN | MEN | CHILDREN

regular price $40.00
on sale $35.00

regular price $39.00
on sale $25.50

all skirts
on sale

regular price $38.99
on sale $30.00

all sweaters
on sale

regular price $69.99
on sale $59.99

B Answer the questions.

1. When is the sale? _____

2. What is the regular price for shoes? _____

3. What is the sale price for shoes? _____

4. What is the sale price for shirts? _____

5. How much can you save on jeans? _____

6. How much can you save on jackets? _____

2 WRITING

A ▶ Listen. Write the information.

Dan's Clothing Store   HOME | SPORTS & LEISURE | BUSINESS | RECREATIONAL

Sale February 16-18

Regular price $35.99

ON SALE _____

Regular price $29.00

ON SALE _____

Regular price $15.50

ON SALE _____

Regular price $52.99

ON SALE _____

Regular price $40.99

ON SALE _____

Regular price $75.00

ON SALE _____

B Read the ad again. Circle *Yes* or *No*.

1. The sale starts on February 18.   Yes   No
2. Sweaters are $35.99 on sale.   Yes   No
3. Pants are $15.99 on sale.   Yes   No
4. T-shirts are $15.50 on sale.   Yes   No
5. Socks and shoes are on sale now.   Yes   No
6. Jackets are on sale on February 16.   Yes   No

C GO ONLINE.

1. Find a sale on a clothing store website.
2. Write the information.

Clothing item: _____   Sale price: _____

I can read store ads. ■   I need more practice. ■

1 | LISTENING

A Look at each picture. What do you see?

B ▶ Listen to the story.

Read and Write About Clothing at a Wedding

2 READING

A ▶ Read and listen.

This is Yun. She lives in the United States. She is getting married.
Her wedding is in August. She needs a new dress. She wants a white dress.
In her native country, people wear white clothes at funerals.
Many women wear a red and green dress at their wedding.
Yun's mother and grandmother want her to have a red and green dress.

B Circle *Yes* or *No*.

1. Yun lives in her native country.	Yes	No
2. Yun's wedding is in October.	Yes	No
3. Yun wants a white dress.	Yes	No
4. In Yun's native country, women wear white dresses at weddings.	Yes	No
5. Yun's grandmother wants Yun to wear a red and green dress.	Yes	No

3 WRITING

A MAKE CONNECTIONS. Talk about clothes in your native country.

1. What color clothes do people wear at funerals?
2. What color dress does a woman wear at her wedding?

B Complete the sentences.

1. In my native country, a woman wears _____ at her wedding.
2. In the United States, a woman wears _____ at her wedding.
3. In my native country, people wear _____ at a funeral.

C WORK TOGETHER. Read your sentences.

I can read and write about clothing at a wedding. ■   I need more practice. ■

Omar is at work.

1 READING

Omar is an assistant manager.
He works at a clothing store.
He helps a customer return clothes.

2 CONVERSATION AT WORK

A Complete the conversation. Write the correct words.

| Omar: | Good afternoon. |
| | _____? |

Customer:	I need to _____ these pants.
Omar:	OK. What's the _____?
Customer:	They are too big.
Omar:	Do you have your receipt?
Customer:	Yes. _____.
Omar:	Thank you.

Can I help you	Here you go
buy	return
problem	question

Here you go	I don't have it

B Practice the conversation.

C Role-play the conversation with new information.

| I can help a customer return clothes. ☐ | I need more practice. ☐ |

VOCABULARY REVIEW

A ► **LISTEN.** Listen and repeat.

beige	black	blue	brown	dress
gray	green	jacket	jeans	orange
pants	pink	purple	red	shirt
shoes	skirt	sneakers	socks	sweater
T-shirt	white	yellow		

B Write the words in the lists.

Colors

_____ _____ _____ _____ _____ _____

_____ _____ _____ _____ _____ _____

Clothing

_____ _____ _____ _____ _____ _____

_____ _____ _____

C **WORK TOGETHER.** Look at the picture. What do you see? Write the colors and the clothes.

1. _____ 2. _____ 3. _____

4. _____ 5. _____ 6. _____

7. _____ 8. _____

D Complete the sentences.

   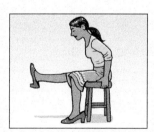

1. The green _____ is _____.

2. The red _____ is _____.

3. The blue _____ are _____.

4. The red _____ are _____.

GRAMMAR REVIEW

A Complete the sentences. Write *this* or *these*.

1. Do you have _____*these*_____ shoes in size 7?

2. Do you have _____ jacket in medium?

3. _____ skirt is too big.

4. _____ shoes are too small.

5. I need to return _____ shirt and _____ pants.

B Complete the sentences. Write *that* or *those*.

1. _____*Those*_____ shirts are on sale.

2. What is the sale price for _____ jacket?

3. Do you like _____ dress?

4. Is _____ T-shirt on sale?

5. Are _____ sweaters on sale?

C Complete the sentences.

Jane	Vic	Tara	Ken	Amy

1. Jane has on _a white shirt and a gray skirt_____.

2. Vic has on _____.

3. Tara has on _____.

4. Ken has on _____.

5. Amy has on _____.

CONVERSATION REVIEW

ROLE-PLAY.

Student A
You are a sales assistant.
You work in a clothing store.
Look at the picture.
Help Student B shop for clothing.

Student B
You are a customer.
You need clothing. You go shopping.
Look at the picture.
Ask for help in the store.

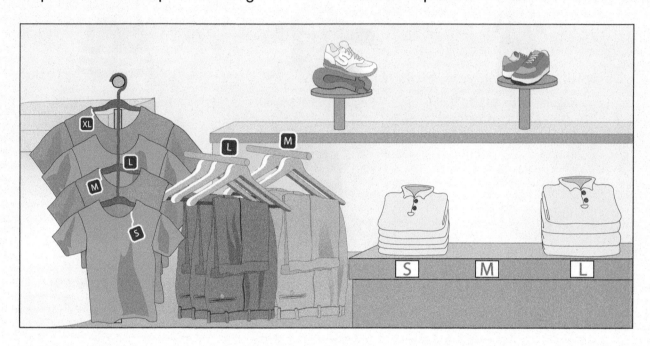

A: Can I help you?

B: Do you have _____?

A: No. I'm sorry. We don't. But we have _____.

B: Do you have _____ in _____?

A: Yes, here you are.

Switch roles.

B: Can I help you?

A: Do you have _____?

B: No. I'm sorry. We don't. But we have _____.

A: Do you have _____ in _____?

B: Yes, here you are.

LIFE SKILLS AND WRITING REVIEW

1 LIFE SKILLS: Read store ads

GOOD LIFE CLOTHING

SALE JUNE 5–19

Regular price: $45.00
On sale: $29.00

Regular price: $60.00
On sale: $40.00

Regular price: $30.00
On sale: $25.00

Regular price: $55.00
On sale: $47.00

Regular price: $69.00
On sale: $45.50

Regular price: $120.99
On sale: $104.99

Read the store ad. Answer the questions.

1. When does the sale start? _____
2. What is the sale price for sneakers? _____
3. How much do you save on sneakers? _____
4. What is the regular price for skirts? _____
5. What is the sale price for jeans? _____
6. What is the regular price for jackets? _____
7. How much do you save on jackets? _____
8. Are sweaters on sale? _____
9. When does the sale end? _____

2 WRITE ABOUT YOURSELF

Answer the question.

Which clothing in the ad do you like?

I like the red jacket. _____

_____

Unit Review: Go back to page 141. Which unit goals can you check off?

9 Our Busy Lives

PREVIEW

Look at the picture. Who do you see?
What is she doing?

UNIT GOALS

- ☐ Talk about what you do for fun
- ☐ Talk about what you are doing
- ☐ Ask about ongoing activities
- ☐ Talk about ongoing activities at work
- ☐ Read and write about weekend schedules
- ☐ **Life skills:** Leave a voicemail
- ☐ **English at work:** Take a personal call

159

Talk About What You Do for Fun

What do you do in your free time?

1 VOCABULARY: Free-time activities

A Look at the pictures. What do you see?

▶ Listen and point. Listen and repeat.

B ▶ Listen and read. Listen and repeat.

1. go online	**2.** play the guitar	**3.** listen to music
4. play soccer	**5.** exercise	**6.** watch TV
7. visit friends	**8.** go to the movies	**9.** play video games

C MAKE CONNECTIONS. What do you do in your free time? Tell your partner.

I play soccer. I go online.

Talk About What You Do for Fun

D ▶ Listen and point. Listen and repeat.

February						
Sunday	Monday	Tuesday	Wednesday	Thursday	Friday	Saturday
1	2	3	4	5	6	⑦
8	9	10	11	12	13	⑭
15	16	17	18	19	20	㉑
22	23	24	25	26	27	㉘

- every Saturday
- once a week

February						
Sunday	Monday	Tuesday	Wednesday	Thursday	Friday	Saturday
1	②	3	④	5	6	7
8	⑨	10	⑪	12	13	14
15	⑯	17	⑱	19	20	21
22	㉓	24	㉕	26	27	28

- every Monday and Wednesday
- twice a week

February						
Sunday	Monday	Tuesday	Wednesday	Thursday	Friday	Saturday
1	②	3	④	5	⑥	7
8	⑨	10	⑪	12	⑬	14
15	⑯	17	⑱	19	⑳	21
22	㉓	24	㉕	26	㉗	28

- every Monday, Wednesday, and Friday
- three times a week

2 CONVERSATION

A ▶ Listen. Listen and repeat.

A: What do you do in your free time?
B: I listen to music. What do you do?
A: I play soccer.
B: How often?
A: Once a week.

B Practice the conversation.

Show what you know!

1. WRITE ABOUT IT. What do you do in your free time? Complete the chart.

Activity	How Often?

2. TALK ABOUT IT. Make new conversations.

A: What do you do in your free time?
B: I _____. What do you do?
A: I _____.
B: How often?
A: _____.

I can talk about what I do for fun. ■	I need more practice. ■

Talk About What You Are Doing

I'm watching a movie.

1 CONVERSATION

A ▶ **Listen. Listen and repeat.**

A: Hello?

B: Hi, Sara. It's Bill. What are you doing?

A: I'm watching a movie. Can I call you later?

B: No problem. Bye.

A: Goodbye.

Sara   Bill

B Practice the conversation.

2 GRAMMAR: Present continuous

I **am** watch**ing** a movie.	**I'm** watch**ing** a movie.
You **are** watch**ing** a movie.	You**'re** watch**ing** a movie.
He **is** watch**ing** a movie.	He**'s** watch**ing** a movie.
She **is** watch**ing** a movie.	She**'s** watch**ing** a movie.
We **are** watch**ing** a movie.	We**'re** watch**ing** a movie.
They **are** watch**ing** a movie.	They**'re** watch**ing** a movie.

A Complete the sentences.

1. I am ____watching____ TV.
             watch

2. She is _____ the guitar.
                play

3. We are _____ to music.
                 listen

4. They are _____ online.
                  go

5. You are _____ video games.
                 play

6. He is _____ friends.
             visit

B Write the answers.

1. **A:** What are you doing?

   B: (I / listen to music) _I'm listening to music._

2. **A:** What is Mrs. White doing?

   B: (she / go online) _____

3. **A:** What are you doing?

   B: (we / visit friends) _____

4. **A:** What's Rob doing?

   B: (he / watch a movie) _____

5. **A:** What are Amy and David doing?

   B: (they / play video games) _____

C ▶ Listen and check your answers. Listen and repeat.

Show what you know!

1. **WRITE ABOUT IT.** Look at the pictures. What are they doing?

1. He's _exercising_____.

2. She's _____.

3. He's _____.

4. They're _____.

2. **TALK ABOUT IT.** What are they doing?

   He's exercising.

| I can talk about what I am doing. ■ | I need more practice. □ |

Ask About Ongoing Activities

Is he doing the laundry?

1 VOCABULARY: Activities at home

A Look at the pictures. What do you see?

▶ Listen and point. Listen and repeat.

B ▶ Listen and read. Listen and repeat.

1. walk the dog	**2.** pay bills	**3.** talk on the phone
4. do homework	**5.** wash the car	**6.** feed the cat

C MAKE CONNECTIONS. What do you do at home?

D WORK TOGETHER. Tell your classmate what you do at home.

2 CONVERSATION

A ▶ Listen. Listen and repeat.

A: Hello?
B: Hi, Jin. How's everything going?
A: Great.
B: Is Alex doing the laundry?
A: Yes, he is.
B: Is Tina washing the car?
A: No, she's not. She's talking on the phone!

Ask About Ongoing Activities

B Practice the conversation.

C WORK TOGETHER. Make new conversations.

A: Hello?

B: Hi, Jin. How's everything going?

A: Great.

B: Is Alex _____?

A: Yes, he is.

B: Is Tina _____?

A: No, she's not. She's _____!

3 GRAMMAR: Present continuous: *Yes / No* questions and answers

Questions	Answers
Are you do**ing** homework?	Yes, **I am.** / No, **I'm not.**
Is Alex do**ing** homework?	Yes, **he is.** / No, **he's not.**
Is Tina do**ing** homework?	Yes, **she is.** / No, **she's not.**
Are the kids do**ing** homework?	Yes, **they are.** / No, **they're not.**

Write questions.

1. (he / make dinner) _Is he making dinner?_ _____

2. (they / play soccer) _____

3. (you / wash the car) _____

4. (Ester / do homework) _____

5. (you / talk on the phone) _____

Show what you know!

1. WRITE ABOUT IT. Write three questions about the pictures on page 164.

_Is he _____?_

2. TELL THE CLASS. Ask your questions.

Is he walking the dog?

I can ask about ongoing activities. ■   I need more practice. ■

She's not helping a customer.

1 VOCABULARY: Workplace activities

A Look at the pictures. What do you see?

▶ Listen and point. Listen and repeat.

B ▶ Listen and read. Listen and repeat.

1. work on the computer	**2.** help a customer	**3.** take a break
4. take orders	**5.** count money	**6.** look for something
7. answer the phone	**8.** drive a truck	**9.** fix cars

C **WORK TOGETHER.** Point to a picture in Exercise A. Say the activity.

Talk About Ongoing Activities at Work

2 GRAMMAR: Present continuous negative

I'm **not** help**ing** a customer.
He**'s not** help**ing** a customer.
She**'s not** help**ing** a customer.
We**'re not** help**ing** a customer.
They**'re not** help**ing** a customer.

A Look at the pictures. Write sentences.

1. (she / drive a truck) _She's driving a truck._
2. (she / help a customer) _She's not helping a customer._

3. (he / count money) _____
4. (he / answer the phone) _____

5. (they / take a break) _____
6. (they / take orders) _____

7. (she / answer the phone) _____
8. (she / fix cars) _____

B ▶ Listen and check your answers. Listen and repeat.

Show what you know!

1. TALK ABOUT IT. Point to a picture on page 166. Make two statements.

She's _____.
She's not _____.

2. WRITE ABOUT IT. Write your statements.

She's looking for something.
She's not answering the phone.

| I can talk about ongoing activities at work. ■ | I need more practice. ■ |

Lesson 5

I'm not coming to work today.

1 VOCABULARY

▶ Listen and read. Listen and repeat.

I'm late for work.

I'm sick.

I can't come to work today.

2 READING

A ▶ Listen and read.

●●●○○ 🛜   **7:28 AM**   33% 🔋

<   **Voicemail**   +

Victor Mata
May 23 at 7:23 AM

▶━●━━━━━━━━

This is Dan Green. Please leave a message.

Transcript
"Hi, Dan. This is Victor Mata. I'm sorry, but I'm not coming to work today. I'm sick."

B Circle *Yes* or *No*.

1. The message is for Dan Green.   Yes   No
2. Victor is calling Dan.   Yes   No
3. Victor is coming to work today.   Yes   No

C ▶ **Listen and read.**

D Circle *Yes* or *No*.

1. The message is for Tanya Smith.   Yes   No
2. Tanya is calling Dan.   Yes   No
3. Tanya is coming to work today.   Yes   No

E **WORK TOGETHER.** Make your own voicemail. Say your sentences.

This is _____. I'm sorry, but _____.

F GO ONLINE.

1. Use your phone to call a classmate or your teacher.
2. Leave a voicemail message.

I can leave a voicemail. ■   I need more practice. ■

Read and Write About Weekend Schedules

This is Luis.

1 LISTENING

A Look at each picture. What do you see?

B ▶ Listen to the story.

Read and Write About Weekend Schedules

2 READING

A ▶ **Read and listen.**

This is Luis. He lives in the United States. He has two children.

His children are busy on weekends. They talk to their friends. They play sports.

Luis and his wife eat alone on weekends. Their children are busy every Saturday and Sunday.

In Luis's native country, families are together on weekends.

They spend time together. They talk.

B **Circle *Yes* or *No*.**

1.	Luis's children are busy every weekend.	Yes	No
2.	Luis plays sports every weekend.	Yes	No
3.	On weekends, his family eats together.	Yes	No
4.	In Luis's native country, families are together on weekends.	Yes	No
5.	Luis spends time with his children on weekends.	Yes	No

3 WRITING

A **MAKE CONNECTIONS.** **Talk about families in your native country.**

1. Are children busy on weekends? What do they do?
2. When do families eat together?
3. When do families spend time together?

B **Complete the sentences.**

1. In my native country, children _____ on weekends.
2. Families _____.
3. In the United States, children _____ on weekends.
4. Families _____.

C **WORK TOGETHER.** **Read your sentences.**

I can read and write about weekend schedules. ■   I need more practice. ■

Pam is at work.

1 READING

Pam is a clerk.
She works in a hotel.
A friend calls her when she is working.

2 CONVERSATION AT WORK

A Complete the conversation. Write the correct words.

Ken: Hi, Pam. It's Ken. _____?

Pam: I'm working right now.

_____?

Ken: Oh! Sorry to bother you.
_____ working tonight?

Pam: No, I'm not. I'm _____ at 5:00.
I can call you then.

Ken: OK, great. Bye!

What are you doing	What do you do
Can I help you	Can I call you later
Are you	Is he
going home	go home

B Practice the conversation.

C Role-play the conversation with new information.

I can take a personal call. ■   I need more practice. ■

A ► **LISTEN. Listen and repeat.**

do homework	drive a truck	exercise
feed the cat	go to the movies	help a customer
pay bills	play soccer	take orders
visit friends	wash the car	work on the computer

B Complete the chart. Use words from Exercise A.

Free-Time Activities	Workplace Activities	Activities at Home

A Look at the pictures. Write sentences. Use contractions.

1. *She's playing the guitar.*

2. _____

3. _____

4. _____

5. _____

6. _____

B Complete the conversations.

1. A: *Are you doing the laundry* _____? (you / do the laundry)
   B: Yes, I am.

2. A: _____? (she / wash the car)
   B: No, she's not.

3. A: Are they paying bills?
   B: Yes, _____.

4. A: Is she listening to music?
   B: No, _____.

5. A: _____? (they / visit friends)
   B: Yes, _____.

C Write sentences.

1. (I / not drive a truck) *I'm not driving a truck.* _____

2. (We / not walk the dog) _____

3. (They / not listen to music) _____

4. (Ella / not play soccer) _____

ROLE-PLAY.

Student A
Look at this picture. Ask questions.

Student B
Answer Student A's questions.

A: What is _____ doing?

B: _____ is _____.

Mario Fang Alice Alex

Student B
Look at this picture. Ask questions.

Student A
Answer Student B's questions.

B: What is _____ doing?

A: _____ is _____.

Mario Fang Alex Alice

1 LIFE SKILLS: Talk about your schedule

A ▶ Listen. Complete the schedule.

●●●○○ 🛜	7:27 PM 33% 🔋
Monday	work, school
Tuesday	_____
Wednesday	work, _____
Thursday	_____
Friday	work, _____
Saturday	soccer
Sunday	_____

B What do you do every week?
Write your activities.

C MAKE CONNECTIONS. Tell your classmates about your activities.

2 WRITE ABOUT YOURSELF

Complete the sentences.

1. My name is _____.
2. Once a week, I _____.
3. Every _____, I _____.
4. I _____ on weekends.

Unit Review: Go back to page 159. Which unit goals can you check off?

10 Where's the Bus Stop?

PREVIEW

Look at the picture. Who do you see?
What is he doing?

UNIT GOALS

- [ ] Ask about places in the community
- [ ] Ask where places are
- [ ] Ask about transportation
- [ ] Ask for and give directions
- [ ] Read and write about transportation
- [ ] **Life skills:** Read traffic signs
- [ ] **English at work:** Give directions

Ask About Places in the Community

Is there a bank near here?

1 VOCABULARY: Places in the community

A Look at the pictures. What do you see?

▶ Listen and point. Listen and repeat.

B ▶ Listen and read. Listen and repeat.

1. a bank	**2.** a drugstore	**3.** a bus stop
4. a restaurant	**5.** an ATM	**6.** a hospital
7. a supermarket	**8.** a convenience store	**9.** a parking lot

C ▶ Listen and look at the map. Point to the streets.

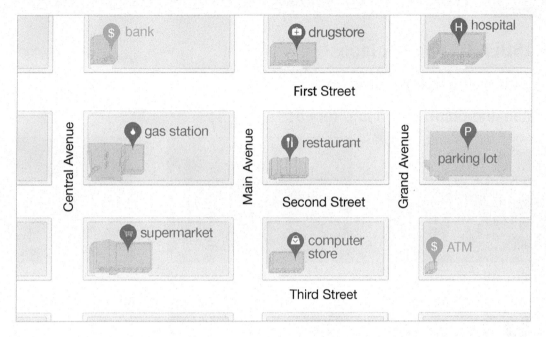

2 CONVERSATION

A ▶ Listen. Listen and repeat.

A: Excuse me. Is there a bank near here?
B: Yes. There's a bank on the corner of First Street and Central Avenue.
A: Thank you.

B Practice the conversation.

Show what you know!

1. TALK ABOUT IT. Look at the map. Make new conversations.

A: Excuse me. Is there _____ near here?
B: Yes. There's _____ on the corner of _____
   and _____.
A: Thank you.

2. WRITE ABOUT IT. Write sentences.

There's a supermarket on the corner of Third Street and Central Avenue.

I can ask about places in the community. ■   I need more practice. ■

Ask Where Places Are

Where is City Hall?

1 VOCABULARY: Public places

A Look at the pictures. What do you see?

▶ Listen and point. Listen and repeat.

B ▶ Listen and read. Listen and repeat.

1. police station	**2.** fire station	**3.** post office
4. library	**5.** park	**6.** courthouse
7. City Hall	**8.** Department of Motor Vehicles (DMV)	**9.** school

C WORK TOGETHER. Point to a place in Exercise A. Say the place.

Ask Where Places Are

2 CONVERSATION

▶ Listen. Listen and repeat. Then practice the conversation.

A: Excuse me. Where is City Hall?

B: It's between the police station and the DMV.

A: Between the police station and the DMV?

B: Yes. And it's across from the park.

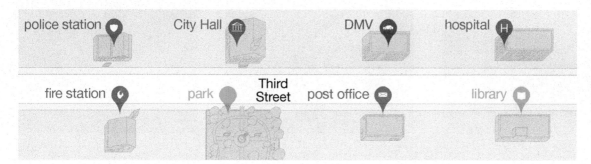

3 GRAMMAR: *Between, across from*

City Hall is **between** the police station and the DMV.   It's **across from** the park.

The post office is **between** the park and the library.   It's **across from** the DMV.

Look at the map. Complete the sentences.

1. The DMV is between _the hospital and City Hall_____.
2. The hospital is across from _____.
3. The park is between _____.
4. The fire station is across from _____.

Show what you know!

1. TALK ABOUT IT. Talk about places in your community.

A: Where is _____?
B: It's _____.

2. WRITE ABOUT IT. Write about places in your community.

The post office is across from the hospital.

I can ask where places are. ■   I need more practice. ■

Ask About Transportation

How do you get to work?

1 VOCABULARY: Getting to work

A Look at the pictures. What do you see?

▶ Listen and point. Listen and repeat.

B ▶ Listen and read. Listen and repeat.

1. walk	**2.** drive	**3.** carpool
4. ride a bike	**5.** take the bus	**6.** take the train
7. take the subway	**8.** take a taxi	**9.** take a ferry

C **MAKE CONNECTIONS.** How do you get to work? Tell a partner.

I walk. I take the bus.

Ask About Transportation

2 CONVERSATION

A ▶ Listen. Listen and repeat.

A: Hi, Ben. Where are you going?
B: I'm going to work.
A: Oh. How do you get to work?
B: I take the bus.

B Practice the conversation.

C ▶ Listen and read.

Ed is a student. He goes to school on Monday and Wednesday. His school is on the corner of White Street and Second Avenue. It's next to the park. He takes the bus to school.

D Circle *Yes* or *No*.

1.	Ed is a student.	Yes	No
2.	Ed goes to school on Monday.	Yes	No
3.	He takes the subway to school.	Yes	No
4.	His school is across from the park.	Yes	No

Show what you know!

1. WRITE ABOUT IT. Ask your partner. Write your partner's information.

A: How do you get to _____?
B: I _____.

Place	Type of Transportation
school	
supermarket	
work	

2. TELL THE CLASS. Talk about your partner.

Manny takes a bus to school. He rides a bike to work.

I can ask about transportation. ■   I need more practice. ■

Ask for and Give Directions

Where is the train station?

1 VOCABULARY: Directions

A ▶ Listen and point. Listen and repeat.

Turn left.   **Go straight.**   **Turn right.**   **Go two blocks.**

B ▶ Listen. Check (✓) the directions you hear.

1. ☐ Go straight.
   ☐ Turn left.
   ☐ Turn right.
   ☐ Go two blocks.

2. ☐ Go straight.
   ☐ Turn left.
   ☐ Turn right.
   ☐ Go two blocks.

3. ☐ Go straight.
   ☐ Turn left.
   ☐ Turn right.
   ☐ Go two blocks.

4. ☐ Go straight.
   ☐ Turn left.
   ☐ Turn right.
   ☐ Go two blocks.

5. ☐ Go straight.
   ☐ Turn left.
   ☐ Turn right.
   ☐ Go two blocks.

6. ☐ Go straight.
   ☐ Turn left.
   ☐ Turn right.
   ☐ Go two blocks.

C ▶ Listen for the directions. Write each place on the map.

bank   hospital   drugstore   post office   school

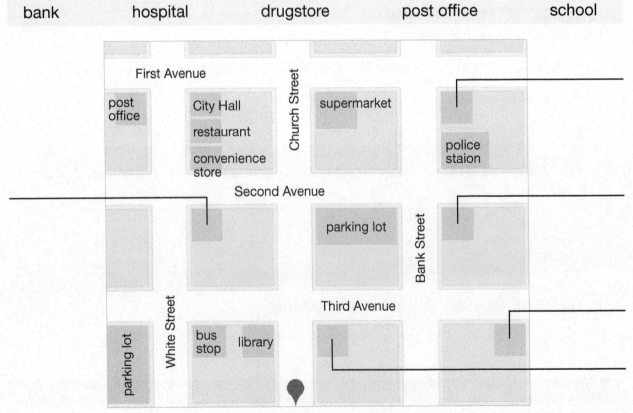

You Are Here

Ask for and Give Directions

2 CONVERSATION

A ▶ Listen. Listen and repeat.

A: Excuse me. Where is the train station?

B: It's on Park Street. Go straight for one block. Then turn left on Park Street.

A: Thanks a lot!

B Practice the conversation.

C WORK TOGETHER. Look at the maps. Make new conversations.

A: Excuse me. Where is the _____?

B: It's on _____. Go straight for _____.

Then turn _____.

A: Thanks a lot!

Conversation 1

Conversation 2

Show what you know!

1. **TALK ABOUT IT.** Ask for and give directions. Use the map on page 184.

   A: Excuse me. Where is _____?
   B: It's _____. Go _____. Then _____.

2. **WRITE ABOUT IT.** Write about the places.

   The post office is on White Street. It's across from City Hall.

I can ask for and give directions. ■   I need more practice. ■

Lesson 5

No parking.

1 VOCABULARY

A ▶ Listen and point. Listen and repeat.

1

stop

2

no left turn

3

walk   don't walk

4

do not enter

5

no parking

6

no U-turn

7

one-way street

8
SPEED LIMIT 25
speed limit 25 miles
per hour

9

crosswalk

B MAKE CONNECTIONS. What signs do you see when you come to class?

C ▶ Listen. Write *1, 2, 3, 4, 5, 6* in the order you hear.

_____

_____

_____

_____

_____

_____

D WORK TOGETHER. Compare your answers.

2 READING

A ▶ Listen. Circle the correct sign.

1.

2.

3.

4. (DO NOT ENTER)   (SPEED LIMIT 25)

B GO ONLINE.

1. Find more traffic signs online.
2. Draw one new sign.
3. Talk about the sign. What does it mean?

I can read traffic signs. ■   I need more practice. ■

1 LISTENING

A Look at each picture. What do you see?

B ▶ Listen to the story.

2 READING

A ▶ **Read and listen.**

This is Mohammed.

In Mohammed's native country, he takes the bus to get to work.

He takes the subway to get to English class.

He takes a taxi to go shopping.

Mohammed lives in the United States. He has a car.

In the United States, Mohammed drives to work. He drives to English class. He drives to go shopping.

B Circle *Yes* or *No*.

1. In his native country, Mohammed takes the bus to get to work.	Yes	No
2. In his native country, he takes a taxi to get to English class.	Yes	No
3. In the United States, Mohammed drives to work.	Yes	No
4. In the United States, Mohammed takes the bus to go shopping.	Yes	No
5. Mohammed has a car in the United States.	Yes	No

3 WRITING

A **MAKE CONNECTIONS.** Talk about how people in your native country get around.

1. Do people take the bus?

2. Do people take the subway?

3. Do people take a taxi?

4. Do people have cars? Do they drive to work?

B Complete the sentences.

1. In my native country, some people _____ to work.

2. In the United States, some people _____ to work.

C **WORK TOGETHER.** Read your sentences.

I can read and write about transportation. ■   I need more practice. ■

English at Work: Give Directions

Ali is at work.

1 READING

Ali is a security guard.
He works at a bank.
He gives directions to a customer.

2 CONVERSATION AT WORK

A Complete the conversation. Write the correct words.

Customer: Excuse me. _____ library?

| Where is the | There is the |

Ali: Go two blocks and turn left. It's _____ the fire station.

| between | across from |

Customer: I'm sorry. Can you repeat that?

Ali: _____. Go two blocks and turn left on Park Street.

| No problem | No, I'm sorry |

Customer: Go two blocks and turn left. I understand. Thank you!

Ali: _____!

| You're welcome | Excuse me |

B Practice the conversation.

C Role-play the conversation with new information.

I can give directions. ■   I need more practice. ■

VOCABULARY REVIEW

A ▶ **LISTEN.** Listen and repeat.

ATM

bank

drugstore

library

police station

supermarket

B Complete the sentences. Use words from Exercise A.

1. A: I need money.

   B: Go to the _____.

2. A: I need food.

   B: Go to the _____.

3. A: I need help.

   B: Go to the _____.

4. A: I need a credit card.

   B: Go to the _____.

5. A: I need soap.

   B: Go to the _____.

6. A: I need a book.

   B: Go to the _____.

C Write the type of transportation.

1. _____

2. _____

3. _____

4. _____

5. _____

6. _____

7. _____

8. _____

GRAMMAR REVIEW

A Write *between, across from,* or *on.*

1. The parking lot is ___across from___ the hospital.

2. City Hall is _____ the post office and the DMV.

3. The hospital is _____ Park Street.

4. The bank is _____ the corner of Second Avenue and Park Street.

5. The courthouse is _____ First Avenue.

```
                        supermarket        police
                                           station
              First Avenue              courthouse
                                           restaurant
                              post
                              office             library
              hospital    parking   City
                            lot      Hall
                                     DMV

              Second Avenue

              bus            bank        school      park
              stop
                            drugstore

              Park Street   Third Avenue   Main Street
```

B Look at the map. Write questions with *Where.*

1. **A:** _Where is the courthouse?_____
   B: It's between the police station and the restaurant.

2. **A:** _____
   B: It's on the corner of First Avenue and Park Street.

3. **A:** _____
   B: It's between the bank and the school.

4. **A:** _____
   B: It's across from the parking lot.

5. **A:** _____
   B: It's across from the bank.

6. **A:** _____
   B: It's on the corner of Second Avenue and Main Street. It's across from the park.

C Complete the conversations. Use *go* or *turn.*

1. **A:** Excuse me. Where is the bus stop?
   B: _____Go_____ straight for one block. Then _____ right.

2. **A:** Where is the library?
   B: _____ left. Then _____ three blocks.

3. **A:** Where is City Hall?
   B: _____ straight for one block. Then _____ left.
   _____ two blocks. It's on Grand Street.

CONVERSATION REVIEW

ROLE-PLAY.

Student A
Ask Student B for directions to:

the hospital
the drugstore
the parking lot

Student B
Look at the map.
Listen to Student A.
Give directions

A: Excuse me. Where is the _____?
B: It's _____. Go _____. Then turn _____.

Student B
Ask Student A for directions to:

the bank
the gas station
the computer store

Student A
Look at the map.
Listen to Student B.
Give directions

B: Excuse me. Where is the _____?
A: It's _____. Go _____. Then turn _____.

LIFE SKILLS AND WRITING REVIEW

1 LIFE SKILLS: Read traffic signs

Look at the pictures. What signs do you see? Write the signs.

1. _____

2. _____

3. _____

4. _____

5. _____

6. _____

2 WRITE ABOUT YOURSELF

Complete the sentences.

1. How do you get to work?

   _____.

2. How do you get to school?

   _____.

3. What signs do you see every day?

   _____.

4. What places in the community do you go to every day?

   _____.

Unit Review: Go back to page 177. Which unit goals can you check off?

11 Get Well Soon

PREVIEW

Look at the picture. Who do you see?
Where are they?

UNIT GOALS

- [ ] Make an appointment
- [ ] Listen to a doctor
- [ ] Offer suggestions
- [ ] Call 911 for emergencies
- [ ] Read and write about a doctor's appointment
- [ ] **Life skills:** Read a medicine label
- [ ] **English at work:** Help someone make an appointment

195

Make an Appointment

My back hurts.

1 VOCABULARY: The body

A Look at the pictures. What do you see?

▶ Listen and point. Listen and repeat.

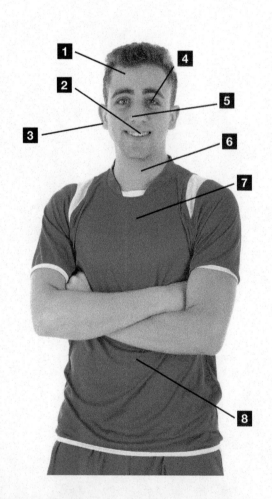
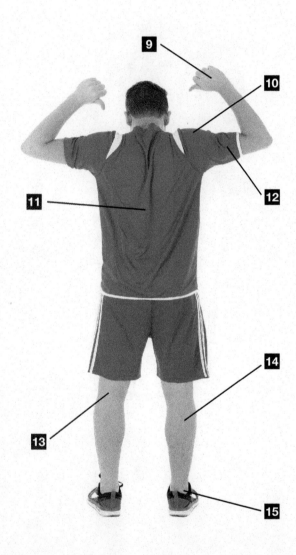

B ▶ Listen and read. Listen and repeat.

1. head	**2.** mouth	**3.** ear	**4.** eye
5. nose	**6.** neck	**7.** chest	**8.** stomach
9. hand	**10.** shoulder	**11.** back	**12.** arm
13. knee	**14.** leg	**15.** foot / feet	

C **WORK TOGETHER.** Point to the pictures. Your partner says the word.

Make an Appointment

2 CONVERSATION

A ▶ **Listen. Listen and repeat.**

Tom

A: Hello. Westside Health Clinic.

B: This is Tom Perez. I'd like to make an appointment.

A: What's the problem?

B: My back hurts.

A: Can you come in at 4:00?

B: Yes, I can.

B Practice the conversation.

C WORK TOGETHER. Make new conversations.

A: Hello. Westside Health Clinic.

B: This is _____. I'd like to make an appointment.

A: What's the problem?

B: My _____ hurts.

A: Can you come in at 4:00?

B: Yes, I can.

Show what you know!

1. **TALK ABOUT IT.** Role-play a conversation.

   Student A has a problem. Call the clinic.
   Student B works at the clinic. Answer the phone. Talk to Student A.

2. **WRITE ABOUT IT.** Perform your conversations for the class.
   Write a sentence about each problem you hear.

   Tom's back hurts.

I can make an appointment. ☐   I need more practice. ☐

Listen to a Doctor

I'm here for a checkup.

1 VOCABULARY: Medical instructions

A Look at the pictures. What do you see?

▶ Listen and point. Listen and repeat.

  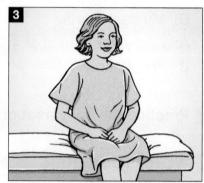

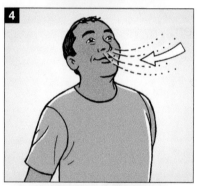  

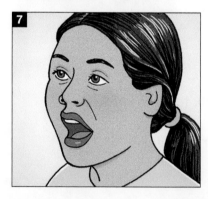 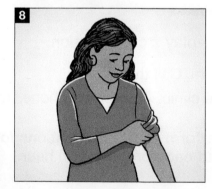 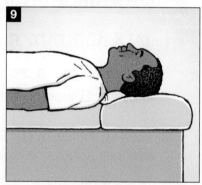

B ▶ Listen and read. Listen and repeat.

1. Take off your jacket.	**2.** Step on the scale.	**3.** Sit on the table.
4. Breathe in.	**5.** Breathe out.	**6.** Look straight ahead.
7. Open your mouth.	**8.** Roll up your sleeves.	**9.** Lie down.

C **WORK TOGETHER.** Tell your partner what to do. Follow your partner's instructions.

Listen to a Doctor

2 CONVERSATION

A ▶ Listen. Listen and repeat.

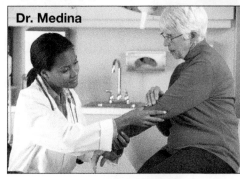
Dr. Medina

A: Hello. I'm Dr. Medina. Why are you here today?
B: I'm here for a checkup.
A: OK. Sit on the table. Look straight ahead.

B Practice the conversation.

C ▶ Listen and read.

Isabel gets a checkup every year. She goes to the health clinic.
Her appointment is on Monday. Her doctor says, "You are healthy."

D Circle *Yes* or *No*.

1. Isabel gets a checkup every year.	Yes	No
2. Isabel has an appointment on Tuesday.	Yes	No
3. Her appointment is at the school.	Yes	No
4. Isabel is sick.	Yes	No

Show what you know!

1. WRITE ABOUT IT. What do you do at the doctor's office?

I step on the scale.

2. TALK ABOUT IT. Tell your partner.

I can listen to a doctor. ■   I need more practice. ■

Offer Suggestions

What's the matter?

1 VOCABULARY: Health problems

A Look at the pictures. What do you see?

▶ Listen and point. Listen and repeat.

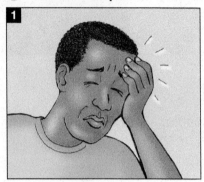 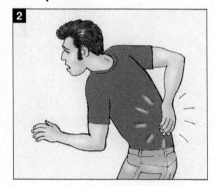 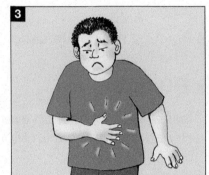

  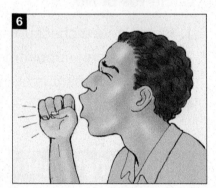

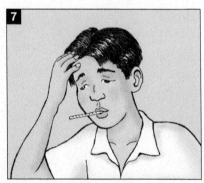  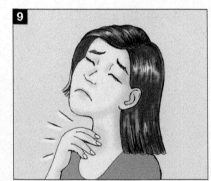

B ▶ Listen and read. Listen and repeat.

1. a headache	**2.** a backache	**3.** a stomachache
4. a toothache	**5.** a cold	**6.** a cough
7. a fever	**8.** the flu	**9.** a sore throat

C **WORK TOGETHER.** Point to a picture. Say the problem. Use *She has* _____ or *He has* _____.

Offer Suggestions

2 CONVERSATION

A ▶ Listen. Listen and repeat.

A: What's the matter?

B: I have a cold.

A: You should drink a lot of liquids.

B Practice the conversation.

3 GRAMMAR: *Should*

 You **should drink** a lot of liquids.

 You **should get** a lot of rest.

 You **should take** aspirin.

 You **should stay** home from work.

Write sentences. Use *should*.

1. you / go to the doctor *You should go to the doctor.*
2. he / get a checkup _____
3. they / take a break _____
4. I / do homework _____
5. we / go online _____
6. you / go to work _____

Show what you know!

1. TALK ABOUT IT. Make new conversations.

A: What's the matter?
B: I have a _____.
A: You should _____.

2. WRITE ABOUT IT. Write your suggestions.

You should drink tea.

I can offer suggestions. ▢   I need more practice. ▢

What's your emergency?

1 VOCABULARY: Emergencies

A Look at the pictures. What do you see?

▶ Listen and point. Listen and repeat.

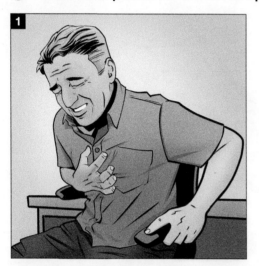

B ▶ Listen and read. Listen and repeat.

1. My friend is having a heart attack.
2. There was a car accident.
3. There is a building on fire.
4. Someone robbed my house.

C **WORK TOGETHER.** Point to a picture. Say the emergency.

Call 911 for Emergencies

2 CONVERSATION

A ▶ Listen. Listen and repeat.

A: 911. What's your emergency?

B: My friend is having a heart attack.

A: Where are you?

B: 1038 Park Avenue.

A: What's the cross street?

B: River Road.

Park Avenue   1038 Park Avenue

B Circle *Yes* or *No*.

1. There is an emergency.	Yes	No
2. Someone is having a heart attack.	Yes	No
3. The emergency is on River Road.	Yes	No
4. The cross street is Park Avenue.	Yes	No

C Practice the conversation.

Show what you know!

1. TALK ABOUT IT. Make new conversations.

A: 911. What's your emergency?

B: _____

A: Where are you?

B: _____

A: What's the cross street?

B: _____

2. TELL THE CLASS. Perform one of your conversations.

I can call 911 for emergencies. ☐   I need more practice. ☐

Life Skills: Read a Medicine Label

Take two teaspoons every four hours.

1 VOCABULARY

A ▶ Listen and read. Listen and repeat.

cough syrup

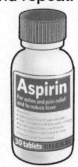

aspirin

prescription medicine

teaspoon

tablets

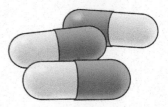

capsules

pills

8:00 a.m.
12:00 p.m.
4:00 p.m.
8:00 p.m.

every 4 hours

8:00 a.m.
2:00 p.m.
8:00 p.m.

every 6 hours

8:00 a.m.
8:00 p.m.

twice a day

B ▶ Listen. Circle the correct words.

Conversation 1

1. The woman is taking ____.
   aspirin
   cough syrup

2. She should take ____.
   2 teaspoons every hour
   2 teaspoons every 4 hours

Conversation 2

3. The man is taking ____.
   prescription medicine
   cough syrup

4. The directions say take 1 capsule ____.
   twice a day with food
   every hour with food

Life Skills: Read a Medicine Label

2 READING

A Read the directions on the label.

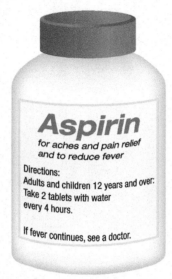

Aspirin
for aches and pain relief
and to reduce fever

Directions:
Adults and children 12 years and over:
Take 2 tablets with water
every 4 hours.

If fever continues, see a doctor.

B Look at the label in Exercise A. Circle the correct words.

1. The medicine is for ___.
coughs   pain and fever

2. Ben has a headache and a fever. He should ___.
take aspirin   take cough syrup

3. Ben is 25 years old. He should ___.
take 2 tablets   take 3 tablets

4. Ben should take the aspirin ___.
every 2 hours   every 4 hours

5. Ben has a fever for 5 days. He should ___.
take more aspirin   see a doctor

C GO ONLINE.

1. Search online for images of medicine labels.
2. Write the instructions.

Name of medicine: _____

Take _____ every _____.

Who should take the medicine? _____

I can read a medicine label. ■   I need more practice. ■

Read and Write About a Doctor's Appointment

This is Teresa.

1 LISTENING

A Look at each picture. What do you see?

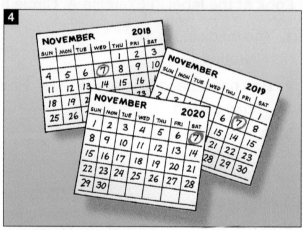

B ▶ Listen to the story.

Read and Write About a Doctor's Appointment

2 READING

A ▶ **Read and listen.**

This is Teresa. She is 45 years old.
In Teresa's native country, people go to the doctor when they are sick.
Teresa lives in the United States. Her daughter wants her to get a checkup.
Her daughter says people should go to the doctor every year.
Teresa feels healthy. She does not want to get a checkup.

B **Circle *Yes* or *No*.**

1. Teresa is 40 years old.	Yes	No
2. In Teresa's native country, people go to the doctor when they are sick.	Yes	No
3. Teresa's daughter does not want her to get a checkup.	Yes	No
4. Teresa's daughter says she should get a checkup every year.	Yes	No
5. Teresa wants to go to the doctor.	Yes	No

3 WRITING

A **MAKE CONNECTIONS.** Talk about doctor's appointments in your native country.

1. How often do people go to the doctor?
2. Do people get a checkup every year?

B **Complete the sentences.**

1. In my native country, people go to the doctor _____.
2. In the United States, people go to the doctor _____.

C **WORK TOGETHER.** Read your sentences.

I can read and write about a doctor's appointment. ■	I need more practice. ■

Unit 11, Lesson 6 **207**

English at Work: Help Someone Make an Appointment

Lila is at work.

Lila

Patient

1 READING

Lila is a nursing assistant.
She works in a clinic.
She helps a patient make an appointment.

2 CONVERSATION AT WORK

A Complete the conversation. Write the correct words.

Lila: Thank you for calling Sunshine Clinic. How can I help you?

Patient: Hello. _____.

I'm here for a checkup	I'd like to make an appointment

Lila: OK. _____?

Patient: My neck hurts. I want to see a doctor.

Can you come in at 3:00	What's the problem

Lila: Of course! _____?

Can you come in at 3:00	What's the problem

Patient: No, I can't. I can come in after 3:30.

Lila: OK. How about 4:00?

Patient: Perfect. Thank you.

Lila: See you then!

B Practice the conversation.

C Role-play the conversation with new information.

I can help someone make an appointment. ■   I need more practice. ■

VOCABULARY REVIEW

A ▶ Listen. Listen and repeat.

arm	back	chest	ear	eye
foot / feet	hand	knee	leg	neck
nose	shoulder	stomach		

B WORK TOGETHER. Point to each part of the body. Say the name.

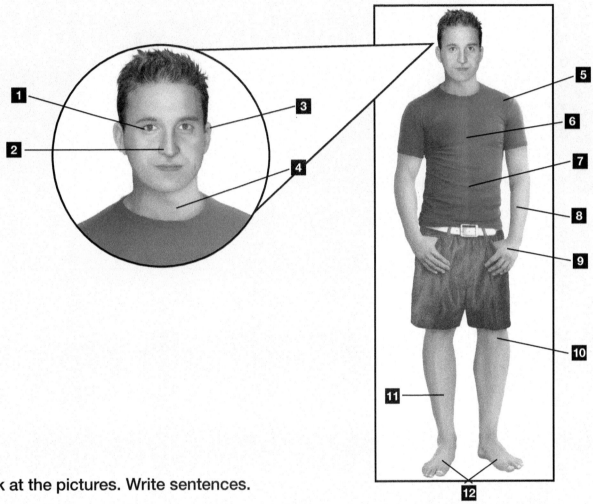

C Look at the pictures. Write sentences.

a cold   a headache   a backache

1. _____   2. _____   3. _____

GRAMMAR REVIEW

A Complete the sentences.

breathe	lie	look	open
roll	sit	~~step~~	take off

1. _____Step_____ on the scale.
2. _____ in.
3. _____ your mouth.
4. _____ straight ahead.
5. _____ up your sleeves.
6. _____ down.
7. _____ your jacket.
8. _____ on the table.

B Write sentences. Use *I'd like to.*

1. (talk to a doctor) _I'd like to talk to a doctor._
2. (make an appointment) _____
3. (talk to a nurse) _____
4. (see a doctor) _____

C Complete the conversations. Make suggestions with *should*.

~~drink liquids~~	stay home from work
take aspirin	take cough medicine

1. **A:** I have a sore throat.
   B: _You should drink liquids._

2. **A:** I have a headache.
   B: _____

3. **A:** I have a cough.
   B: _____

4. **A:** I have the flu.
   B: _____

ROLE-PLAY.

Student A
You don't feel well.
You have a headache and a cough.

Student B
You are Student A's friend.
Give suggestions.

A: What's the matter?

B: I have _____.

A: You should _____.

Student B
You don't feel well.
You have the flu and a stomachache.

Student A
You are Student B's friend.
Give suggestions.

B: What's the matter?

A: I have _____.

B: You should _____.

1 | LIFE SKILLS: Read a medicine label

Read the label. Then complete the sentences and answer the questions.

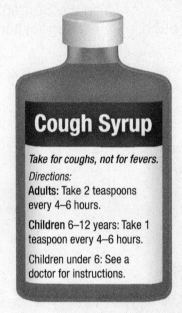

Cough Syrup

Take for coughs, not for fevers.

Directions:
Adults: Take 2 teaspoons every 4–6 hours.

Children 6–12 years: Take 1 teaspoon every 4–6 hours.

Children under 6: See a doctor for instructions.

1. What medicine is it? _____

2. Adults should take _____ teaspoons.

3. Adults should take the medicine _____ hours.

4. A 12-year-old child should take _____.

5. A 12-year-old child should take the medicine _____ hours.

6. Your child is 5. What should you do?
_____

2 | WRITE ABOUT YOURSELF

Answer the questions.

1. What do you do for a sore throat? _____

2. What do you do for a headache? _____

3. What do you do for a cough? _____

4. What do you do for a cold? _____

Unit Review: Go back to page 195. Which unit goals can you check off?

12 What Do You Do?

PREVIEW

Look at the picture. Who do you see?
What is she doing?

UNIT GOALS

- [ ] Say your occupation
- [ ] Ask about someone's job
- [ ] Talk about job skills
- [ ] Apply for a job

- [ ] Read and write about a job interview
- [ ] **Life skills:** Read a job ad
- [ ] **English at work:** Apply for a new job

Say Your Occupation

I'm a teacher's assistant.

1 VOCABULARY: Jobs

A Look at the pictures. What do you see?

▶ Listen and point. Listen and repeat.

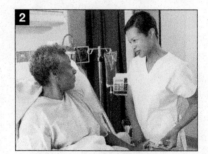

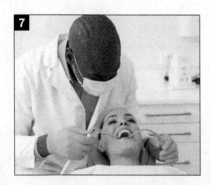

B ▶ Listen and read. Listen and repeat.

1. a mechanic	**2.** a nursing assistant	**3.** a painter
4. a construction worker	**5.** a teacher's assistant	**6.** a sales assistant
7. a dentist	**8.** a housekeeper	**9.** a bus driver

C **WORK TOGETHER.** Point to a picture. Your partner says the job.

Say Your Occupation

2 CONVERSATION

A ▶ Listen. Listen and repeat.

A: Let's get coffee.
B: I'm sorry. I can't. I have to go to work.
A: Oh. What do you do?
B: I'm a teacher's assistant.

B Practice the conversation.

C **WORK TOGETHER.** Make new conversations. Use the jobs on page 214.

A: Let's get coffee.
B: I'm sorry. I can't. I have to go to work.
A: Oh. What do you do?
B: I'm a _____.

Show what you know!

1. **TALK ABOUT IT.** Ask classmates: *What do you do?*
   Write the information.

Name	Job
Omar	mechanic

2. **WRITE ABOUT IT.** Write sentences.

Omar is a mechanic.

I can say my occupation. ◻   I need more practice. ◻

Ask About Someone's Job

Where does he work?

1 VOCABULARY: More jobs

A Look at the pictures. What do you see?

▶ Listen and point. Listen and repeat.

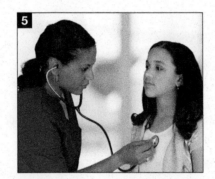

B ▶ Listen and read. Listen and repeat.

1. a cashier	**2.** a doctor	**3.** a factory worker
4. a cook	**5.** a nurse	**6.** an office assistant
7. a security guard	**8.** a server	**9.** a custodian

C **WORK TOGETHER.** Point to a picture. Say the job.

Ask About Someone's Job

2 CONVERSATION

A ▶ Listen. Listen and repeat.

A: Who's that?
B: That's Bo. He's a nurse.
A: Where does he work?
B: He works at Valley Hospital.

Bo

B Practice the conversation.

3 GRAMMAR: *Where do, where does*

Where do you work?	**Where does** he work?
Where do they work?	**Where does** she work?

Complete the conversations. Write *do* or *does*.

1. **A:** Where _____*does*_____ Gino work?
   B: He works at a café.

2. **A:** Where _____ you work?
   B: I work at a restaurant.

3. **A:** Where _____ Yuki work?
   B: She works at home.

4. **A:** Where _____ Ivan work?
   B: He works at a school.

5. **A:** Where _____ Hannah and Sasha work?
   B: They work at a hotel.

Show what you know!

1. **TALK ABOUT IT.** Ask about your partner.

   What do you do?
   Where do you work?

2. **TELL THE CLASS.** Talk about your partner.

   Mina is a cook. She works in a restaurant.

I can ask about someone's job. ■   I need more practice. ■

Talk About Job Skills

What are your job skills?

1 VOCABULARY: Job skills

Ⓐ Look at the pictures. What do you see?

▶ Listen and point. Listen and repeat.

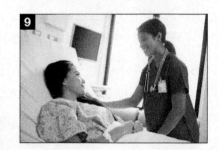

Ⓑ ▶ Listen and read. Listen and repeat.

1. speak two languages	**2.** use a cash register	**3.** help customers
4. use a computer	**5.** use office machines	**6.** build houses
7. fix something	**8.** operate machinery	**9.** take care of patients

Ⓒ **WORK TOGETHER.** Point to a picture. Say the job skill.

Talk About Job Skills

2 CONVERSATION

A ▶ Listen. Listen and repeat.

A: What are your job skills?
B: I can use a computer.
    And I can use a cash register.
A: What other skills do you have?
B: I can speak two languages.

B Practice the conversation.

C ▶ Listen and read.

Grace needs a new job. She has an interview on Wednesday. Grace has many skills. She can use a computer and a cash register. Grace can also speak two languages.

D Circle *Yes* or *No*.

1. Grace wants a new job.	Yes	No
2. She has an interview on Monday.	Yes	No
3. Grace can use a cash register.	Yes	No
4. She can speak three languages.	Yes	No

Show what you know!

1. WRITE ABOUT IT. What are your job skills?

I can _____. And I can _____.

2. TALK ABOUT IT. Ask about your partner's job skills.

A: What are your job skills?
B: I can use a computer. And I can speak two languages.

I can talk about job skills. ☐   I need more practice. ☐

Apply for a Job

I'd like to apply for the office assistant job.

1 CONVERSATION

A ▶ **Listen. Listen and repeat.**

A: Hello. I'd like to apply for the office assistant job.

B: OK. Can you use a computer?

A: Yes, I can.

B: Please fill out the application.

A: Thank you.

B Circle *Yes* or *No*.

1. The man wants a mechanic job.   Yes   No
2. The man can use a computer.   Yes   No
3. The man should fill out the application.   Yes   No

C Practice the conversation.

C **WORK TOGETHER.** Read the job ads. Make new conversations.

A: Hello. I'd like to apply for the _____ job.

B: OK. Can you _____?

A: Yes, I can.

B: Please fill out the application.

A: Thank you.

Conversation 1

● ● ●

Mechanic needed to fix cars

Conversation 2

● ● ●

Sales assistant needed to help customers

Conversation 3

● ● ●

Construction worker needed to build houses

Apply for a Job

2 GRAMMAR: *Can*

Can you **use** a computer?	**Yes**, I **can**. **No**, I **can't**.
Can Mr. Vega **use** a computer?	**Yes**, he **can**. **No**, he **can't**.
Can Nancy **use** a computer?	**Yes**, she **can**. **No**, she **can't**.
Can Alex and Chris **use** a computer?	**Yes**, they **can**. **No**, they **can't**.

A Write the questions and answers.

1. **A:** _Can Miss Tang serve customers?_ (can / Miss Tang / serve customers)
   B: Yes, _____she can_____.

2. **A:** _____ (can / Mr. Black / use a computer)
   B: No, _____.

3. **A:** _____ (can / you / build houses)
   B: Yes, _____.

4. **A:** _____ (can / Marina and Pedro / help customers)
   B: Yes, _____.

5. **A:** _____ (can / Ella / speak two languages)
   B: No, _____.

B ▶ Listen and check your answers. Listen and repeat.

Show what you know!

1. **TALK ABOUT IT.** Ask: *Can you* _____? Check (✓) your partner's job skills.

   ☐ speak two languages   ☐ use office machines
   ☐ take care of patients   ☐ use a cash register
   ☐ use a computer   ☐ fix things

2. **WRITE ABOUT IT.** Write sentences about your partner.

   Trina can use a cash register and a computer.

I can apply for a job. ■	I need more practice. ■

I can work with a team.

1 VOCABULARY

A Complete the sentences. Use words from the box.

apply online	full-time	go in person	part-time	required	weekdays	weekends

1. I work 15 hours a week. I work _____.
2. I work 40 hours a week. I work _____.
3. I work on Saturdays and Sundays. I work _____.
4. I work Monday to Friday. I work _____.
5. I have to go to the office for my interview. I have to _____.
6. I need to have experience for this job. Experience is _____.
7. I need to fill out an application on a website. I have to _____.

B ▶ Listen and read. Listen and repeat.

I can work with a team.

I can work independently.

I can communicate well.

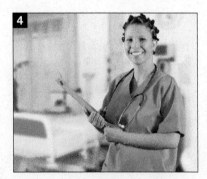

I have a positive attitude.

I manage my time well.

I can work under pressure.

Life Skills: Read a Job Ad

2 READING

A MAKE CONNECTIONS. What skills do you have?

I manage my time well.

B Read the job ads.

Help Wanted
Sales Assistant
1 year experience required
Must work well under pressure
Full-time evenings and
  weekends
Apply online: BestStores.com

A

Job Available
Cashier
No experience required
Must communicate well and
  work with a team
Part-time 25 hours / week
Call Ella Lopez: 616-555-9543

B

Driver Needed
Full-time 35 hours / week
2 years experience required
Must work independently
Apply in person:
ABC Company
300 Plaza Avenue

C

C Match the sentences with the ads. Write *A, B,* or *C.*

1. This job is full-time evenings and weekends. _____
2. You need two years of experience. _____
3. You need to work with a team. _____
4. You need to apply in person. _____
5. This job is 35 hours a week. _____
6. You need to work well under pressure. _____
7. You need to work independently. _____
8. You need to apply online. _____

D GO ONLINE.

1. Find a job ad online.
2. Write the skills you need for the job.

I can read a job ad. ■   I need more practice. ■

A Look at each picture. What do you see?

B ▶ Listen to the story.

Read and Write About a Job Interview

2 READING

A ► Read and listen.

This is Monika. She lives in the United States.
Monika has a job interview on Thursday at 9:00.
Monika is ready for the interview. She practiced her interview skills in her English class.
Monika gets to the interview. She is early. She says hello and smiles.
She shakes hands with Mr. Cruz.
Mr. Cruz asks about Monika's job skills. She answers his questions.

B Circle *Yes* or *No*.

1. Monika has a job interview on Tuesday.   Yes   No
2. She practiced her interview skills.   Yes   No
3. She gets to the interview early.   Yes   No
4. She hugs Mr. Cruz.   Yes   No
5. She answers Mr. Cruz's questions.   Yes   No

3 WRITING

A **MAKE CONNECTIONS.** Talk about job interviews in your native country.

1. Do people arrive on time for job interviews?
2. Do people practice their interview skills?
3. Do people shake hands with the interviewer?

B Complete the sentences.

1. In my native country, people arrive _____ for job interviews.
2. They _____ with the interviewer.
3. In the United States, people arrive _____ for job interviews.
4. They _____ with the interviewer.

C **WORK TOGETHER.** Read your sentences.

I can read and write about a job interview. ■   I need more practice. ■

Van is at work.

Van   Manager

1 READING

Van is a mechanic.
He works at a car repair shop.
He wants to apply for a new job.

2 CONVERSATION AT WORK

A Complete the conversation. Write the correct words.

Van:	Hello. _____ the job.
Manager:	OK. Do you have experience?
Van:	Yes, I do. I work at Tom's Cars now.
	I have five years of _____.
Manager:	That's great! When _____?
Van:	I can start next week!
Manager:	OK. Please _____.
Van:	Thank you! I can do it now.

I'd like to apply for	I want
experience	attitude
do you work	can you begin work
apply in person	fill out an application

B Practice the conversation.

C Role-play the conversation with new information.

I can apply for a new job. ■   I need more practice. ■

VOCABULARY REVIEW

A ▶ **Listen. Listen and repeat.**

build houses	cashier	communicate well	doctor
drive a truck	fix something	help customers	housekeeper
manage time well	mechanic	nurse	office assistant
sales assistant	server	speak two languages	take care of patients
teacher	teacher's assistant	use a computer	work with a team

B Complete the chart. Use words from Exercise A.

Jobs	Skills

C Match the jobs and the skills.

_____ **1.** cashier   **a.** take care of patients

_____ **2.** construction worker   **b.** drive a truck

_____ **3.** nurse   **c.** use a cash register

_____ **4.** office assistant   **d.** build houses

_____ **5.** truck driver   **e.** use a computer

GRAMMAR REVIEW

A **Write questions. Use *Where do* or *Where does*.**

1. (he / work) _Where does he work?_

2. (she / go to school) _____

3. (you / work) _____

4. (they / apply for the job) _____

5. (Emmy / drive a truck) _____

B **Write questions and answers. Use *can*.**

1. A: (you / use a computer) _Can you use a computer?_

   B: Yes, _I can_ .

2. A: (she / speak two languages) _____

   B: No, _____ .

3. A: (Tom / drive a truck) _____

   B: No, _____ .

4. A: (they / build houses) _____

   B: Yes, _____ .

5. A: (Laura / take care of patients) _____

   B: Yes, _____ .

6. A: (you / use a cash register) _____

   B: No, _____ .

ROLE-PLAY.

Student A
Apply for a server job. You can:

- help customers
- speak two languages
- work under pressure

Student B
Ask about Student A.

A: Hello. I'm interested in the _____ position.

B: OK. What job skills do you have?

A: _____

B: Do you have any other skills?

A: _____

B: When can you work?

A: _____

B: Please fill out this application.

A: OK. Thank you.

Student B
Apply for an office assistant job. You can:

- use a computer
- use office machines
- work with a team

Student A
Ask about Student B.

B: Hello. I'm interested in the _____ position.

A: OK. What job skills do you have?

B: _____

A: Do you have any other skills?

B: _____

A: When can you work?

B: _____

A: Please fill out this application.

B: OK. Thank you.

LIFE SKILLS AND WRITING REVIEW

1 LIFE SKILLS: Fill out a job application

What kind of job are you interested in? Fill out the application.

POSITION APPLYING FOR: _____

PERSONAL INFORMATION

NAME _____ _____
        First   Last

ADDRESS _____
        Street

_____ ___ ___
        City   State ZIP Code

___ - ___ - ___
Phone Number

Are you 18 years or older? ○ Yes ○ No

AVAILABILITY

When can you begin work? ___ ___ ___
                         Month Day Year

Are you interested in a full-time job or a part-time job?
○ FT   ○ PT

2 WRITE ABOUT YOURSELF

Complete the sentences.

1. My name is _____.
2. I'd like to apply for _____.
3. I can begin work _____.
4. I can work _____ hours a week.

Unit Review: Go back to page 213. Which unit goals can you check off?

WORD LIST

UNIT 1

Cambodia, 6
Canada, 6
China, 6
eight, 10
El Salvador, 6
five, 10

four, 10
Haiti, 6
Mexico, 6
nine, 10
one, 10
Peru, 6

seven, 10
six, 10
Somalia, 6
South Korea, 6
student, 14
Syria, 6

teacher, 14
three, 10
two, 10
United States, 6
Vietnam, 6
zero, 10

UNIT 2

across from, 35
ask questions, 38
backpack, 28
book, 28
bookstore, 32
cafeteria, 32
classmates, 38
classroom, 32
close, 30
computer lab, 32

dictionary app, 28
eraser, 28
go to class, 38
library, 32
married, 36
Miss, 36
Mr. (mister), 36
Mrs. (missus), 36
Ms. (miss), 36
next to, 34

notebook, 28
office, 32
open, 30
paper, 28
pen, 28
pencil, 28
phone, 28
practice with my
    classmates, 38
put away, 30

read signs, 38
restroom, 32
single, 36
take out, 30
testing room, 32
turn off, 30
turn on, 30
use a dictionary app, 38
write new words, 38

UNIT 3

eat breakfast, 52
eat lunch, 52
Friday, 54
get dressed, 52
get home, 52

get up, 52
go to school, 52
go to sleep, 52
go to work, 52
Monday, 54

numbers 0–59, 48
rest, 56
Saturday, 54
Sunday, 54
take a shower, 52

Thursday, 54
Tuesday, 54
Wednesday, 54

UNIT 4

April, 72
August, 72
brother, 66
children, 66
clean the house, 70
daughter, 66
December, 72
do the laundry, 70
fall, 72

father, 66
February, 72
grandfather, 66
grandmother, 66
husband, 66
January, 72
July, 72
June, 72
make dinner, 70

March, 72
May, 72
months, 72
mother, 66
November, 72
October, 72
parents, 66
seasons, 72
September, 72

sister, 66
son, 66
spring, 72
summer, 72
take out the garbage, 70
vacuum, 70
wash the dishes, 70
wife, 66
winter, 72

UNIT 5

aspirin, 90
batteries, 90
card, 94
cents, 92
deodorant, 90
dime, 86
dollar, 88

enter your PIN, 94
half-dollar, 86
insert your card, 94
light bulbs, 90
nickel, 86
paper towels, 90
penny, 86

quarter, 86
razors, 90
remove your card, 94
shampoo, 90
shaving cream, 90
sign your name, 94
soap, 90

swipe your card, 94
tap OK, 94
tissues, 90
toilet paper, 90
toothpaste, 90

UNIT 6

apples, 108
bag, 111
baked potato, 114
bananas, 108
box, 111
can, 111
carrots, 104
cereal, 114
cheeseburger, 114
cherries, 108

chicken sandwich, 114
coffee, 114
cucumbers, 104
dozen, 111
eggs and toast, 114
French fries, 114
fruit salad, 114
gallon, 111
grapes, 108
green salad, 114

iced tea, 114
juice, 114
lettuce, 104
loaf, 111
mangoes, 108
mushrooms, 104
onions, 104
oranges, 108
pancakes, 114
peaches, 108

pears, 108
peas, 104
peppers, 104
potatoes, 104
pound, 110
rice, 114
strawberries, 108
tea, 114
tomatoes, 104
tuna fish sandwich, 114

UNIT 7

avenue, 130
basement, 124

bathroom, 124
bed, 128

bedroom, 124
boulevard, 130

chair, 128
closet, 124

dining room, 124
dishwasher, 128
dresser, 128
drive, 130
dryer, 128
garage, 124
kitchen, 124

lamp, 128
lane, 130
large, 126
laundry room, 124
living room, 124
new, 126
refrigerator, 128

road, 130
shower, 128
sink, 128
small, 126
sofa, 128
stove, 128
street, 130

sunny, 126
table, 128
toilet, 128
washing machine, 128

UNIT 8

beige, 146
black, 146
blue, 146
brown, 146
dress, 142
extra large, 144
gray, 146

green, 146
jacket, 142
jeans, 142
large, 144
medium, 144
orange, 146
pants, 142

pink, 146
purple, 146
red, 146
shirt, 142
shoes, 142
skirt, 142
small, 144

sneakers, 142
socks, 142
sweater, 142
T-shirt, 142
white, 146
yellow, 146

UNIT 9

answer the phone, 166
count money, 166
do homework, 164
drive a truck, 166
exercise, 160
feed the cat, 164
fix cars, 166

go online, 160
go to the movies, 160
help a customer, 166
late, 168
listen to music, 160
look for something, 166
pay bills, 164

play soccer, 160
play the guitar, 160
play video games, 160
sick, 168
take a break, 166
take orders, 166
talk on the phone, 164

visit friends, 160
walk the dog, 164
wash the car, 164
watch TV, 160
work on the computer, 166

UNIT 10

ATM, 178
bank, 178
bus stop, 178
carpool, 182
City Hall, 180
convenience store, 178
courthouse, 180
crosswalk, 186
Department of Motor
   Vehicles (DMV), 180
do not enter, 186

don't walk, 186
drive, 182
drugstore, 178
fire station, 180
go straight, 184
go two blocks, 184
hospital, 178
library, 180
no left turn, 186
no parking, 186
no U-turn, 186

one-way street, 186
park, 180
parking lot, 178
police station, 180
post office, 180
restaurant, 178
ride a bike, 182
school, 180
speed limit, 186
stop sign, 186
supermarket, 178

take a ferry, 182
take a taxi, 182
take the bus, 182
take the subway, 182
take the train, 182
turn left, 184
turn right, 184
walk, 182, 186

UNIT 11

arm, 196
aspirin, 204
back, 196
backache, 200
breathe in, 198
breathe out, 198
capsules, 204
car accident, 202
chest, 196
cold, 200
cough, 200

cough syrup, 204
ear, 196
eye, 196
feet, 196
fever, 200
fire, 202
flu, 200
foot, 196
hand, 196
head, 196
headache, 200

heart attack, 202
knee, 196
leg, 196
lie down, 198
look straight ahead, 198
mouth, 196
neck, 196
nose, 196
open your mouth, 198
pills, 204
prescription medicine, 204

rob, 202
roll up your sleeves, 198
shoulder, 196
sit on the table, 198
sore throat, 200
step on the scale, 198
stomachache, 200
tablets, 204
take off your jacket, 198
teaspoon, 204
toothache, 200

UNIT 12

apply online, 222
build houses, 218
bus driver, 214
cashier, 216
communicate well, 222
construction worker, 214
cook, 216
custodian, 216
dentist, 214
doctor, 216

factory worker, 216
fix something, 218
full-time, 222
help customers, 218
housekeeper, 214
in person, 222
independently, 222
manage time, 222
mechanic, 214
nurse, 216

nursing assistant, 214
office assistant, 216
operate machinery, 218
painter, 214
part-time, 222
positive attitude, 222
required, 222
sales assistant, 214
security guard, 216
server, 216

speak two languages, 218
take care of patients, 218
teacher's assistant, 214
team, 222
use a cash register, 218
use a computer, 218
use office machines, 218
weekdays, 222
weekends, 222
work under pressure, 222

AUDIO SCRIPT

UNIT 1

Page 7, Conversation, Exercise A

A: Hello. My name is Rick Soto.
B: Hi. I'm May Chen.
A: Where are you from, May?
B: I'm from China.

Page 8, Vocabulary, Exercise B

1. C
2. F
3. H
4. J
5. M
6. P
7. R
8. U
9. X
10. Z
11. L
12. Q

Page 8, Vocabulary, Exercise D

1. hello, h-e-l-l-o
2. my, m-y
3. name, n-a-m-e
4. where, w-h-e-r-e
5. are, a-r-e
6. from, f-r-o-m

Page 9, Conversation, Exercise A

A: What's your name, please?
B: Ana Sol.
A: Spell your first name.
B: A-N-A.
A: Spell your last name.
B: S-O-L.

Page 10, Vocabulary, Exercise B

a. 0
b. 2
c. 5
d. 6
e. 8
f. 9

Page 10, Vocabulary, Exercise C

1. The student ID is 02468.
2. The student ID is 65378.
3. The student ID is 05376.

Page 11, Conversation, Exercise A

A: What's your student ID number?
B: 83241.
A: 83241?
B: That's right.

Page 11, Conversation, Exercise C

A: What's your phone number?
B: 212-555-7169.
A: 212-555-7169?
B: That's right.

Page 11, Conversation, Exercise E

1. 231-555-7283
2. 434-555-0516

Page 11, Conversation, Exercise F

1. 813-555-6291
2. 325-555-0478
3. 714-555-3924

Page 12, Grammar, Exercise C

1. I'm a student.
2. You're the teacher.
3. You're from Peru.
4. I'm from the United States.
5. I'm from Syria.
6. You're my classmate.

Page 13, Conversation, Exercise A

A: Hello. I'm Rosa.
B: Hi. I'm Rick. Nice to meet you.
A: Nice to meet you, too.

Page 14, Conversation, Exercise A

A: This is Jin Su. He is from Korea.
B: Hi, Jin Su. I'm Lora.
C: Nice to meet you.
B: Nice to meet you, too.

Page 16, Conversation, Exercise A

A: Who are they?
B: Oscar and Carlos. They're my classmates.
A: Where are they from?
B: They're from Brazil.

Page 18, Reading, Exercise A

first name
middle name
last name
phone number
place of birth
student ID number

Page 20, Listening, Exercise B
Page 21, Reading, Exercise A

This is Ivan. He is a student.

He says hello to his classmates and smiles.

In his school, some students say hello and shake hands.

Some students say hello and hug.
Some students say hello and bow.
Other students say hello and kiss.

UNIT 2

Page 29, Conversation, Exercise A

A: Excuse me. Do you have a pencil?
B: No, I don't.
A: Do you have a pen?
B: Yes, I do. Here you go.
A: Thanks.

Page 31, Conversation, Exercise A

A: It is time for a test. Please close your books.
B: OK.
A: Use a pencil. Don't use a pen.

Page 31, Grammar, Exercise B

1. Don't open your backpack.
2. Don't use a dictionary app.
3. Don't put away your notebook.
4. Don't turn off your phone.
5. Don't take out your book.
6. Don't close the door.

Page 33, Conversation, Exercise A

A: Where is the teacher?
B: He's in the library.

Page 33, Conversation, Exercise D

1. Where is the teacher?
   He's in the computer lab.
2. Where is Sara?
   She's in the library.
3. Where is your book?
   It's in the cafeteria.
4. Where is your backpack?
   It's in the classroom.

Page 34, Conversation, Exercise A

A: Excuse me. Where is the bookstore?
B: It's next to the testing room.
A: Thanks.

Page 35, Conversation, Exercise A

A: Excuse me. Where is the library?
B: It's across from the office.
A: Thanks.

Page 36, Vocabulary, Exercise B

1. Mrs. Chen
2. Mr. Smith
3. Ms. Lopez
4. Miss Park

Page 36, Reading, Exercise A

Mr.
Mrs.
Miss
Ms.
last name
first name
place of birth
female
male
class
teacher

Page 38, Conversation, Exercise A

A: How do you study English?
B: I practice with my classmates, and I write new words.
A: That's great!

Page 40, Listening, Exercise B
Page 41, Reading, Exercise A

This is Lan.
In her native country, students do not talk in class.
They listen to the teacher.
In the United States, students talk in groups.
Students ask questions.
The teacher listens to the students.

UNIT 3

Page 48, Vocabulary, Exercise C

a. 20
b. 19
c. 24
d. 13
e. 15
f. 14
g. 26
h. 27

Page 49, Conversation, Exercise A

A: What time is it?
B: It's 1:00.

Page 50, Conversation, Exercise A

A: What time is your English class?
B: It's from 9:00 to 12:30.
A: What time is your break?
B: It's from 10:45 to 11:15.

Page 53, Conversation, Exercise A

A: What time do you go to work?
B: I go to work at 6:00. What time do you go to work?
A: I go to work at 10:00.

Page 54, Conversation, Exercise A

A: When do you work, Nora?
B: I work from Monday to Friday.
A: When do you go to school?
B: I go to school on Saturday.
A: You're really busy!

Page 54, Conversation, Exercise C

Hi, I'm Nora. I'm very busy. I work from Monday to Friday. I go to school on Saturday. I go to the library on Sunday.

Page 55, Grammar, Exercise B

1. I work from Monday to Thursday.
2. We play soccer on Tuesday.
3. I go to school on Friday.
4. They go to school from Wednesday to Friday.
5. I eat lunch at home on Sunday.

Page 58, Listening, Exercise B
Page 59, Reading, Exercise A

Manny gets up at 6:00.

He gets to work at 7:55. He starts work at 8:00. He is on time.

He goes to school after work.

He gets to class at 5:45. Class starts at 6:00. He is early.

Manny meets friends on Saturday. But he is late!

Page 61, Vocabulary Review, Exercise A

1. 46
2. 16
3. 81
4. 25
5. 38
6. 73
7. 2
8. 57
9. 11
10. 99

UNIT 4

Page 67, Conversation, Exercise A

A: Who's that?
B: That's my brother.
A: What's his name?
B: Sam.
A: Who's that?
B: That's my sister.
A: What's her name?
B: Her name is Tina.

Page 68, Conversation, Exercise A

A: Do you have any sisters or brothers?
B: Yes. I have two sisters and one brother.
A: That's nice. Do you have any children?
B: No, I don't.

Page 68, Reading, Exercise A

Hi, I'm Marta. This is my family. That's my husband. His name is Pedro. My parents are Linda and Roberto. I have two sons, Ernesto and Tino. I have one daughter. Her name is Ana.

Page 69, Grammar, Exercise A

one brother, two brothers
a sister, three sisters
one son, two sons
a daughter, three daughters
one parent, two parents
one child, two children

Page 71, Conversation, Exercise A

A: Do you vacuum?
B: Yes, I do.
A: Do you make dinner?
B: No, I don't.

Page 72, Vocabulary, Exercise B

1. December
2. June
3. October
4. January
5. May
6. April

Page 73, Conversation, Exercise A

A: What's your favorite season?
B: Summer.
A: That's nice. My favorite season is spring.

Page 74, Vocabulary, Exercise D

1. February 23, 1994
2. July 14, 2015
3. September 2, 2009
4. January 11, 2019
5. September 7, 1974

AUDIO SCRIPT

Page 75, Conversation, Exercise A

A: What is today's date?
B: April 9, 2019.
A: Thanks.

Page 76, Reading, Exercise A

first name
middle name
last name
today's date
date of birth
place of birth
class
teacher
class schedule
day
time
room

Page 78, Listening, Exercise B
Page 79, Reading, Exercise A

Lucas and Carla are married. Lucas is Carla's husband. Carla is Lucas's wife.

In their native country, men go to work.

In their native country, women do the household chores.

In the United States, Carla and Lucas go to work.

They both do household chores. Lucas washes the dishes.

Lucas goes to the supermarket, too.

Page 81, Vocabulary Review, Exercise B

1. January
2. February
3. March
4. April
5. May
6. June
7. July
8. August
9. September
10. October
11. November
12. December

UNIT 5

Page 86, Conversation, Exercise A

A: Excuse me. Do you have change for a dollar?
B: Yes. I have two quarters and five dimes. Here you go.
A: Thanks.

Page 87, Conversation, Exercise D

1. Do you have change for a dollar?
   Yes. I have three quarters, two dimes, and a nickel.
2. Do you have change for a dollar?
   Yes. I have two quarters, four dimes, and two nickels.
3. Do you have change for a quarter?
   Yes. I have a dime and three nickels.
4. Do you have change for a quarter?
   Yes. I have two dimes and five pennies.

Page 89, Conversation, Exercise A

A: Excuse me. Do you have change for a ten?
B: Yes. I have a five and five ones. Here you go.
A: Great.

Page 89, Conversation, Exercise D

1. Do you have change for a five?
   Yes. I have five ones.
2. Do you have change for a twenty?
   Yes. I have two tens.
3. Do you have change for a fifty?
   Yes. I have two twenties and two fives.
4. Do you have change for a hundred?
   Yes. I have a fifty, two twenties, and a ten.

Page 91, Grammar, Exercise B

1. Where is the shampoo?
2. Where are the paper towels?
3. Where is the shaving cream?
4. Where are the light bulbs?
5. Where are the batteries?

Page 92, Vocabulary, Exercise B

1. It's 17 cents.
2. It's 36 cents.
3. It's 44 cents.
4. It's 60 cents.
5. It's 79 cents.
6. It's 95 cents.

Page 92, Vocabulary, Exercise D

1. It's $1.25.
2. It's $3.07.
3. It's $4.79.
4. It's $7.50.
5. It's $8.99.
6. It's $10.42.
7. It's $12.55.
8. It's $15.35.
9. It's $17.95.

Page 93, Conversation, Exercise A

A: Excuse me. How much is the toothpaste?
B: It's $3.99.
A: How much are the batteries?
B: They're $4.50.
A: Thanks.

Page 96, Listening, Exercise B
Page 97, Reading, Exercise A

This is Edna. In her native country, she shops at a market.

She talks about the price. She asks for a better price.

She is happy.

In the United States, Edna shops in a big store.

Each item has one price.

Edna pays a good price in the United States, too. She buys things on sale.

UNIT 6

Page 105, Conversation, Exercise A

A: Hi. I'm at the store. Do we need vegetables?
B: Yes. We need tomatoes and carrots.
A: OK. Do we need onions?
B: No. We have onions.

Page 105, Conversation, Exercise D

Hi, I'm Pam. It's time to make vegetable soup! I have tomatoes, onions, peas, and potatoes. I need mushrooms and carrots.

Page 106, Conversation, Exercises A, B, and C

A: Do you like vegetables?
B: I like tomatoes. I don't like onions. What about you?
A: I like peppers. I don't like carrots.

Page 109, Conversation, Exercise A

A: Does your daughter like fruit?
B: She likes apples. She doesn't like pears.

Page 110, Vocabulary

bananas, one ninety-nine a pound
grapes, three seventy-nine a pound
fish, eight ninety-nine a pound
ground beef, five eighty-nine a pound
chicken, four thirty-nine a pound

Page 110, Conversation, Exercise A

A: Do you need anything from the store?
B: Yes. I need one pound of grapes and two pounds of ground beef.

Page 111, Conversation, Exercise A

A: What do we need from the store?
B: We need a bag of rice and two dozen eggs.

Page 112, Reading, Exercise A

Shop Mart Weekly Specials
a loaf of bread, $1.79
one dozen eggs, $1.29
chicken, $1.99 a pound
tomato soup, 79 cents. buy one, get one free.
cereal, $4.25
bananas, 49 cents a pound

Page 115, Conversation, Exercise A

A: Are you ready to order?
B: Yes. I'd like a tuna fish sandwich, a green salad, and an iced tea.
A: Anything else?
B: No, thank you.

Page 116, Listening, Exercise B
Page 117, Reading, Exercise A

This is Tran. In his native country, most people eat with chopsticks.

Many children eat with their hands.

This is Riko. In her native country, many people drink soup.

In the United States, most people eat with a fork, knife, and spoon.

They eat sandwiches and French fries with their hands.

Page 122, Life Skills Review, Exercise A

a bag of rice
a dozen eggs
a pound of ground beef
two pounds of chicken

UNIT 7

Page 125, Conversation, Exercise A

A: Guess what? I have a new apartment.
B: Really? What's it like?
A: It has a kitchen, a living room, and one bedroom.
B: It sounds great!

AUDIO SCRIPT

Page 126, Conversation, Exercise A

A: Can you tell me about the apartment for rent?

B: There is a sunny bedroom, a new kitchen, and a large living room.

A: It sounds nice.

Page 129, Conversation, Exercise A

A: I have some questions about the apartment. Is there a refrigerator?

B: Yes, there is.

A: Are there any lamps?

B: No, there aren't.

Page 129, Grammar, Exercise B

1. Is there a stove?
   Yes, there is.

2. Are there any chairs?
   Yes, there are.

3. Are there any lamps?
   No, there aren't.

4. Is there a washing machine?
   No, there isn't.

Page 130, Vocabulary, Exercise B

1. 270 John Lane
2. 15 City Street
3. 1460 Third Avenue
4. 60 Park Drive
5. 319 Sun Boulevard

Page 130, Vocabulary, Exercise C

1. 75 Sandy Boulevard
2. 1325 West Avenue
3. 5 Main Street
4. 836 Jones Road
5. 1514 North Drive
6. 26 Town Lane

Page 131, Conversation, Exercise A

A: I'm looking for an apartment.

B: Oh! There's an apartment for rent on my street.

A: What's the address?

B: It's 1630 River Street.

A: How much is the rent?

B: It's $900 a month.

Page 134, Listening, Exercise B
Page 135, Reading, Exercise A

This is Pilar. She is 21 years old. She is single.

Pilar lives with her sister and her sister's husband.

Pilar has a good job. She works in an office.

Pilar wants to live with her friends. In the United States, many single people live with friends.

Pilar's parents are not happy. In their native country, single people live with their families.

UNIT 8

Page 143, Conversation, Exercise A

A: Let's go shopping! I need a new jacket.

B: OK. I need new shoes.

Page 144, Conversation, Exercise A

A: Can I help you?

B: Do you have this shirt in large?

A: Yes. Here you go.

B: Do you have these pants in size 12?

A: No, I'm sorry. We don't.

Page 147, Conversation, Exercise A

A: Is Nina here?

B: Yes. She's over there.

A: Where? What does she have on?

B: She has on a red shirt and black pants.

A: OK. Thanks.

Page 148, Vocabulary, Exercise B

1. This shirt is too big.
2. Those pants are too small.
3. This dress is too big.
4. Those sneakers are too small.

Page 148, Conversation, Exercise A

A: I need to return this jacket and these shoes.

B: What's the problem?

A: The jacket is too big. The shoes are too small. Here's my receipt.

Page 151, Writing, Exercise A

Dan's Clothing Store.

Sale! February 16–18.

Sweaters, regular price $35.99, on sale for $25.99.

Pants, regular price $29, on sale for $15.99.

T-shirts, regular price $15.50, on sale for $10.

Shoes, regular price $52.99, on sale for $45.

Sneakers, regular price $40.99, on sale for $25.

Jackets, regular price $75, on sale for $50.

Page 152, Listening, Exercise B

Page 153, Reading, Exercise A

This is Yun. She lives in the United States. She is getting married.

Her wedding is in August. She needs a new dress. She wants a white dress.

In her native country, people wear white clothes at funerals.

Many women wear a red and green dress at their wedding.

Yun's mother and grandmother want her to have a red and green dress.

UNIT 9

Page 161, Conversation, Exercise A

A: What do you do in your free time?
B: I listen to music. What do you do?
A: I play soccer.
B: How often?
A: Once a week.

Page 162, Conversation, Exercise A

A: Hello?
B: Hi, Sara. It's Bill. What are you doing?
A: I'm watching a movie. Can I call you later?
B: No problem. Bye.
A: Goodbye.

Page 163, Grammar, Exercise C

1. What are you doing?
   I'm listening to music.
2. What is Mrs. White doing?
   She's going online.
3. What are you doing?
   We're visiting friends.
4. What's Rob doing?
   He's watching a movie.
5. Ware are Amy and David doing?
   They're playing video games.

Page 164, Conversation, Exercise A

A: Hello?
B: Hi, Jin. How's everything going?
A: Great.
B: Is Alex doing the laundry?
A: Yes, he is.
B: Is Tina washing the car?
A: No, she's not. She's talking on the phone!

Page 167, Grammar, Exercise B

1. She's driving a truck.
2. She's not helping a customer.
3. He's counting money.
4. He's not answering the phone.
5. They're taking a break.
6. They're not taking orders.
7. She's answering the phone.
8. She's not fixing cars.

Page 168, Reading, Exercise A

A: This is Dan Green. Please leave a message.
B: Hi, Dan. This is Victor Mata. I'm sorry, but I'm not coming to work today. I'm sick.

Page 169, Reading, Exercise C

A: This is Dan Green. Please leave a message.
B: Hi, Dan. This is Tanya Smith. I'm sorry, but I'm late for work. My bus is late.

Page 170, Listening, Exercise B

Page 171, Reading, Exercise A

This is Luis. He lives in the United States. He has two children.

His children are busy on weekends. They talk to their friends. They play sports.

Luis and his wife eat alone on weekends. Their children are busy every Saturday and Sunday.

In Luis's native country, families are together on weekends.

They spend time together. They talk.

Page 176, Life Skills Review, Exercise A

Monday: work, school
Tuesday: work
Wednesday: work, school
Thursday: work
Friday: work, movies
Saturday: soccer
Sunday: make dinner

UNIT 10

Page 179, Vocabulary, Exercise C

First Street
Second Street
Third Street
Central Avenue
Main Avenue
Grand Avenue

Page 179, Conversation, Exercise A

A: Excuse me. Is there a bank near here?
B: Yes. There's a bank on the corner of First Street and Central Avenue.
A: Thank you.

Page 181, Conversation

A: Excuse me. Where is City Hall?
B: It's between the police station and the DMV.
A: Between the police station and the DMV?
B: Yes. And it's across from the park.

Page 183, Conversation, Exercise A

A: Hi, Ben. Where are you going?
B: I'm going to work.
A: Oh. How do you get to work?
B: I take the bus.

Page 183, Conversation, Exercise C

Ed is a student. He goes to school on Monday and Wednesday. His school is on the corner of White Street and Second Avenue. It's next to the park. He takes the bus to school.

Page 184, Vocabulary, Exercise B

1. Where the bank?
   It's on Park Street. Go straight for one block.
2. Where's the post office?
   It's between the DMV and City Hall. Turn left on Third Street.
3. Where's the school?
   It's on Lake Street. Turn right at the corner.
4. Where's the hospital?
   It's on First Street. Turn right at the corner.
5. Where's the convenience store?
   Turn left at the bank. It's next to the drugstore.
6. Where's the police station?
   Go two blocks. It's across from the park.

Page 184. Vocabulary, Exercise C

1. Is there a bank near here?
   Yes. Go straight. It's on the corner of Third Avenue and Church Street.
2. Where's the hospital?
   Go straight for three blocks and turn right. It's on the corner of First Avenue and Bank Street.
3. Where's the drugstore?
   Go to Third Avenue and turn right at the corner. Go straight for two blocks.
4. Is there a post office near here?
   Yes. Go straight for two blocks. Turn right at the corner. It's on the corner of Second Avenue and Bank Street.

5. Is there a school near here?
   Go straight for two blocks. Turn left at the corner. It's on the corner of Second Avenue and White Street.

Page 185, Conversation, Exercise A

A: Excuse me. Where is the train station?
B: It's on Park Street. Go straight for one block. Then turn left on Park Street.
A: Thanks a lot!

Page 187, Vocabulary, Exercise C

1. no parking
2. no U-turn
3. crosswalk
4. stop
5. do not enter
6. speed limit 25 miles per hour

Page 187, Reading, Exercise A

1. Only go one way on this street.
2. Don't walk across the street.
3. Stop at the corner.
4. Drive 25 miles per hour.

Page 188, Listening, Exercise B
Page 189, Reading, Exercise A

This is Mohammed.

In Mohammed's native country, he takes the bus to get to work.

He takes the subway to get to English class.

He takes a taxi to go shopping.

Mohammed lives in the United States. He has a car.

In the United States, Mohammed drives to work. He drives to English class. He drives to go shopping.

UNIT 11

Page 197, Conversation, Exercise A

A: Hello. Westside Health Clinic.
B: This is Tom Perez. I'd like to make an appointment.
A: What's the problem?
B: My back hurts.
A: Can you come in at 4:00?
B: Yes, I can.

Page 199, Conversation, Exercise A

A: Hello. I'm Dr. Medina. Why are you here today?
B: I'm here for a checkup.
A: OK. Sit on the table. Look straight ahead.

Page 199, Conversation, Exercise C

Isabel gets a checkup every year. She goes to the health clinic. Her appointment is on Monday. Her doctor says, "You are healthy."

Page 200, Vocabulary, Exercises A and B

a headache
a backache
a stomachache
a toothache
a cold
a cough
a fever
the flu
a sore throat

Page 201, Conversation, Exercise A

A: What's the matter?
B: I have a cold.
A: You should drink a lot of liquids.

Page 203, Conversation, Exercise A

A: 911. What's your emergency?
B: My friend is having a heart attack.
A: Where are you?
B: 1038 Park Avenue.
A: What's the cross street?
B: River Road.

Page 204, Vocabulary, Exercise B

Conversation 1
Are you OK? You have a bad cough.
I know. I'm taking cough syrup.
How much are you taking?
I'm taking two teaspoons every four hours.
I hope you feel better soon.

Conversation 2
Hi, Mike. How are you?
I don't feel well. I have a fever and an ear infection.
Oh that's too bad. Are you taking medicine?
Yes. I'm taking some prescription medicine.
That's good. How often do you take it?
I have to take one capsule twice a day with food.
I hope you feel better soon.

Page 206, Listening, Exercise B
Page 207, Reading, Exercise A

This is Teresa. She is 45 years old.

In Teresa's native country, people go to the doctor when they are sick.

Teresa lives in the United States. Her daughter wants her to get a checkup.

Her daughter says people should go to the doctor every year.

Teresa feels healthy. She does not want to get a checkup.

UNIT 12

Page 215, Conversation, Exercise A

A: Let's get coffee.
B: I'm sorry. I can't. I have to go to work.
A: Oh. What do you do?
B: I'm a teacher's assistant.

Page 217, Conversation, Exercise A

A: Who's that?
B: That's Bo. He's a nurse.
A: Where does he work?
B: He works at Valley Hospital.

Page 219, Conversation, Exercise A

A: What are your job skills?
B: I can use a computer. And I can use a cash register.
A: What other skills do you have?
B: I can speak two languages.

Page 219, Conversation, Exercise C

Grace needs a new job. She has an interview on Wednesday. Grace has many skills. She can use a computer and a cash register. Grace can also speak two languages.

Page 220, Conversation, Exercise A

A: Hello. I'd like to apply for the office assistant job.
B: OK. Can you use a computer?
A: Yes, I can.
B: Please fill out the application.
A: Thank you.

Page 221, Grammar, Exercise B

1. Can Miss Tang serve customers?
   Yes, she can.

2. Can Mr. Black use a computer?
   No, he can't.

3. Can you build houses?
   Yes, I can.

4. Can Marina and Pedro help customers?
   Yes, they can.

5. Can Ella speak two languages?
   No, she can't.

AUDIO SCRIPT

Page 224, Listening, Exercise B

Page 225, Reading, Exercise A

This is Monika. She lives in the United States.

Monika has a job interview on Thursday at 9:00.

Monika is ready for the interview. She practiced her interview skills in her English class.

Monika gets to the interview. She is early. She says hello and smiles.

She shakes hands with Mr. Cruz.

Mr. Cruz asks about Monika's job skills. She answers his questions.

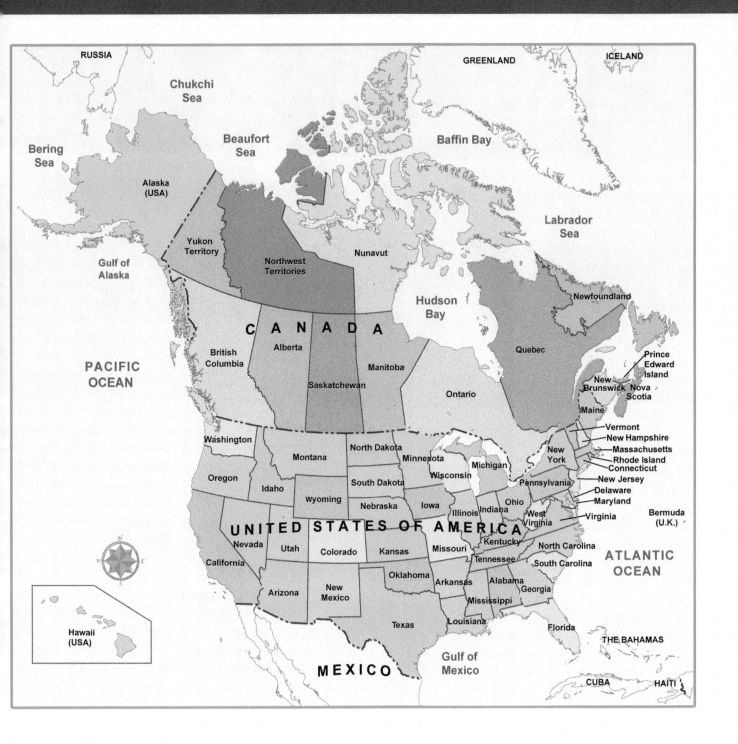

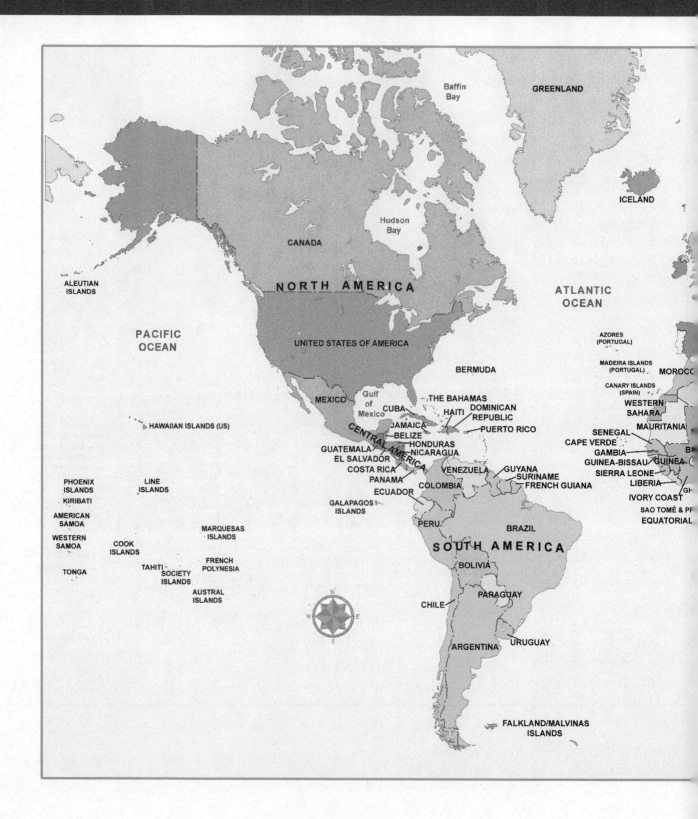

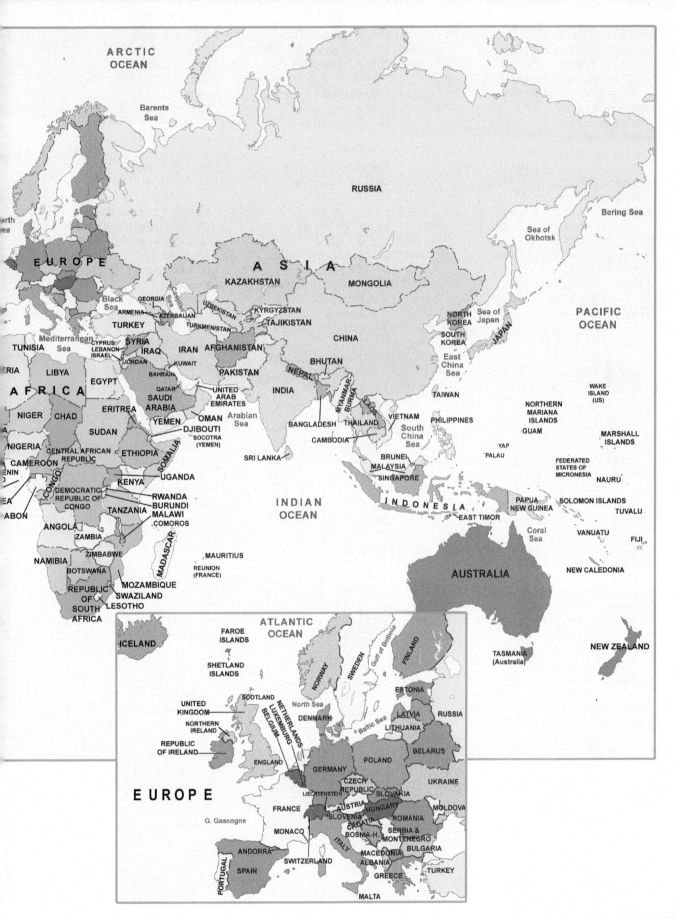

ARCTIC
OCEAN

Barents
Sea

RUSSIA

Bering Sea

Sea of
Okhotsk

EUROPE

ASIA

KAZAKHSTAN

MONGOLIA

PACIFIC
OCEAN

Black
Sea

GEORGIA

ARMENIA

Caspian Sea

UZBEKISTAN

KYRGYZSTAN

AZERBAIJAN

TURKMENISTAN

TAJIKISTAN

NORTH
KOREA

Sea of
Japan

TURKEY

CHINA

JAPAN

SOUTH
KOREA

Mediterranean
Sea

CYPRUS
LEBANON
ISRAEL

SYRIA

IRAQ

IRAN

AFGHANISTAN

NEPAL

East
China
Sea

TUNISIA

JORDAN

KUWAIT

TAIWAN

LIBYA

EGYPT

BAHRAIN

PAKISTAN

BHUTAN

WAKE
ISLAND
(US)

ERIA

QATAR

SAUDI
ARABIA

UNITED
ARAB
EMIRATES

INDIA

MYANMAR,
BURMA

LAOS

NORTHERN
MARIANA
ISLANDS

AFRICA

NIGER

CHAD

ERITREA

YEMEN

OMAN

Arabian
Sea

BANGLADESH

THAILAND

VIETNAM

PHILIPPINES

GUAM

MARSHALL
ISLANDS

SUDAN

DJIBOUTI

SOCOTRA
(YEMEN)

CAMBODIA

South
China
Sea

YAP

NIGERIA

CENTRAL AFRICAN
REPUBLIC

ETHIOPIA

SOMALIA

SRI LANKA

BRUNEI

PALAU

CAMEROON

MALAYSIA

FEDERATED
STATES OF
MICRONESIA

NAURU

ENIN

CONGO

UGANDA

SINGAPORE

ABON

DEMOCRATIC
REPUBLIC OF
CONGO

KENYA

RWANDA
BURUNDI

INDONESIA

PAPUA
NEW GUINEA

SOLOMON ISLANDS

A

TANZANIA

MALAWI

INDIAN
OCEAN

EAST TIMOR

TUVALU

ANGOLA

COMOROS

ZAMBIA

MADAGASCAR

Coral
Sea

VANUATU

FIJI

NAMIBIA

ZIMBABWE

MAURITIUS

NEW CALEDONIA

BOTSWANA

REUNION
(FRANCE)

AUSTRALIA

REPUBLIC
OF
SOUTH
AFRICA

MOZAMBIQUE

SWAZILAND

LESOTHO

ATLANTIC
OCEAN

TASMANIA
(Australia)

NEW ZEALAND

ICELAND

FAROE
ISLANDS

Gulf of Bothnia

FINLAND

SHETLAND
ISLANDS

NORWAY

SWEDEN

ESTONIA

SCOTLAND

North Sea

RUSSIA

UNITED
KINGDOM

NETHERLANDS
LUXEMBURG
BELGIUM

DENMARK

LATVIA

NORTHERN
IRELAND

Baltic Sea

LITHUANIA

REPUBLIC
OF IRELAND

ENGLAND

BELARUS

GERMANY

POLAND

EUROPE

LIECHTENSTEIN

CZECH
REPUBLIC

UKRAINE

SLOVAKIA

G. Gascogne

FRANCE

AUSTRIA
SLOVENIA

HUNGARY

MOLDOVA

MONACO

CROATIA
BOSNIA-H.

ROMANIA

SERBIA &
MONTENEGRO

ANDORRA

ITALY

MACEDONIA

BULGARIA

PORTUGAL

SPAIN

SWITZERLAND

ALBANIA

TURKEY

GREECE

MALTA

INDEX

INDEX

CREDITS

Photos:

Front cover: Front cover: Westend61/Getty Images; Bjoern Lauen/ArabianEye/Getty Images; Hero Images/Getty Images; Manuel Breva Colmeiro/Moment/Getty Images.

Frontmatter

Page vi (cellphone): Tele52/Shutterstock; vi (front cover): Westend61/Getty Images; vi (front cover): Bjoern Lauen/ArabianEye/Getty Images; vi (front cover): Hero Images/Getty Images; vi (front cover): Manuel Breva Colmeiro/Moment/Getty Images; vi (MyEnglishLab screenshot): Pearson Education Inc.; vi (ActiveTeach screenshot): Pearson Education Inc.; vi (CCRS page, bottom left): Wavebreakmedia/Shutterstock; vi (CCRS page, top right): Illustration Forest/Shutterstock; vi Wavebreak Media Ltd/123RF (Active Teach page); vii: Siri Stafford/DigitalVision/Getty Images; viii (left, p. 66): Shutterstock; viii (right, p. 67): Dmytro Zinkevych/123RF; ix (p. 68): Wavebreak Media Ltd/123RF; x (p. 76): rSnapshotPhotos/Shutterstock; xiii (p. 81 [1]): Kirill Kedrinski/123RF; xiii (p. 81 [2]): Maskot/Getty Images; xiii (p. 81 [3]): Andriy Popov/123RF; xiii (p. 81 [4]): Hongqi Zhang/123RF; xiii (p. 81 [5]): Elena Elisseeva/Shutterstock; xiii (p. 81 [6]): Andriy Popov/123RF; xiii (p. 83): Cathy Yeulet/123RF; xxii: Courtesy of Sarah Lynn; xxii: Courtesy of Ronna Magy; xxii: Courtesy of Federico Salas Isnardi.

Pre-unit: Welcome to Class

Page 4: Tele52/Shutterstock.

Unit 1

Page 5: Dolgachov/123RF; 7: Thomas Barwick/DigitalVision/Getty Images; 9: AshTproductions/Shutterstock; 10 (John Pace): Comstock/Stockbyte/Getty Images; 10 (John Potter): Joe Belanger/Shutterstock; 10 (Sue Gao): Fuse/Corbis/Getty Images; 10 (Grace Tang): Ariwasabi/123RF; 10 (Anne Joseph): OLJ Studio/Shutterstock; 10 (Anne Crane): Arek_Malang/Shutterstock; 11: Jörg Carstensen/Pearson Education Ltd; 12 (left): Original Photography by David Mager; 12 (right): Original Photography by David Mager; 13: Blend Images/Shutterstock; 14 (A, left): Elwynn/123RF; 14 (A, right): Iofoto/Shutterstock; 14 (B, 1): Tracy Whiteside/Shutterstock; 14 (B, 2): Simon Greig/Shutterstock; 14 (B, 3): Leungchopan/Shutterstock; 14 (B, 4): Shutterstock; 14 (B, 5): Phase4Studios/Shutterstock; 14 (B, 6): SnowWhiteimages/Shutterstock; 14 (bottom, right): James Hardy/PhotoAlto/Alamy Stock Photo; 15 (1): Christopher Meder/Shutterstock; 15 (2): Darrin Henry/123RF; 15 (3): Blend Images/Shutterstock; 15 (4): Mimagephotography/Shutterstock; 16 (1): Original Photography by David Mager; 16 (2): Original Photography by David Mager; 16 (3): Original Photography by David Mager; 23 (1): Cathy Yeulet/123RF; 23 (2): David Gilder/Shutterstock; 23 (3): OLJ Studio/Shutterstock; 25: Sirtravelalot/Shutterstock.

Unit 2

Page 27: Robert Kneschke/Shutterstock; 28 (1): Rabia Elif Aksoy/123RF; 28 (2): Bondarchuk/Shutterstock; 28 (3): Valkr/Shutterstock; 28 (4): Joe Belanger/Shutterstock; 28 (5): Binik/Shutterstock; 28 (6): Weerachai Ruttanasopa/Shutterstock; 28 (7): Vitaly Korovin/123RF; 28 (8): Olegdudko/123RF; 28 (9): J. Helgason/Shutterstock; 29: VP Photo Studio/Shutterstock; 31: Wavebreakmedia/Shutterstock; 32 (1): Wavebreakmedia/Shutterstock; 32 (2): Trekandshoot/Shutterstock; 32 (3): Jack Hollingsworth/Photodisc/Getty Images; 32 (4): Dumrongsak/123RF; 32 (5): Sakaekrung/Shutterstock; 32 (6): Hotsum/Shutterstock; 32 (7): Mint Images/Getty Images; 32 (8): Picsfive/123RF; 33: Wavebreak Media Ltd/123RF; 36 (left, top): Stylephotographs/123RF; 36 (left, bottom): Blend Images/123RF; 38 (1): Rabia Elif Aksoy/123RF; 38 (2): Maskot/Getty Images; 38 (3): Wavebreak Media Ltd/123RF; 38 (4): Frederic Cirou/PhotoAlto/Alamy Stock Photo; 38 (5): ESB Professional/Shutterstock; 38 (6): Clynt Garnham Education/Alamy Stock Photo; 38 (bottom, left): Michaeljung/Shutterstock; 39: Blend Images/Shutterstock; 43 (1): Fotocrisis/Shutterstock; 43 (2): Ekaphon Maneechot/Shutterstock; 43 (3): Newphotoservice/Shutterstock; 43 (4): Kongsak Yonyot/123RF; 43 (5): Bryljaev/123RF; 43 (6): Cheuk-King Lo/Pearson Education Asia Ltd; 43 (7): Jean-Marie Guyon/123RF; 43 (8): John Arehart/Shutterstock.

Unit 3

Page 47: Mangostar/Shutterstock; 48 (D): Maxfromhell/Shutterstock; 50 (top, left): Frederic Cirou/PhotoAlto Agency RF Collections/Getty Images; 50 (top, center): Klaus Vedfelt/DigitalVision/Getty Images; 50 (bottom, right): Ammentorp/123RF; 52 (1): Lightwavemedia/Shutterstock; 52 (2): Di Studio/Shutterstock; 52 (3): FLUKY FLUKY/Shutterstock; 52 (4): Zohaib Hussain/Getty Images; 52 (5): Dolgachov/123RF; 52 (6): Wong Yu Liang/Shutterstock; 52 (7): Stieberszabolcs/123RF; 52 (8): Shutterstock; 52 (9): Andriy Popov/123RF; 53 (top, left): John M Lund Photography Inc/DigitalVision/Getty Images; 53 (top, right): Lena Mirisola/Image Source/

Getty Images; 54: Wavebreak Media Ltd/123RF; 56 (top, left): Tele52/Shutterstock; 56 (top, right): Cathy Yeulet/123RF; 57: Tele52/Shutterstock; 61 (1): Wavebreak Media Ltd/123RF; 61 (2): Di Studio/Shutterstock; 61 (3): S_L/Shutterstock; 61 (4): Cathy Yeulet/123RF; 61 (5): Darrin Henry/Shutterstock; 61 (6): Cathy Yeulet/123RF.

Unit 4

Page 65: Siri Stafford/DigitalVision/Getty Images; 66: Shutterstock; 67: Dmytro Zinkevych/123RF; 68: Wavebreak Media Ltd/123RF; 70 (1): Torwai Suebsri/123RF; 70 (2): Dinis Tolipov/123RF; 70 (3): Thanapol Kuptanisakorn/123RF; 70 (4): Andriy Popov/123RF; 70 (5): Andriy Popov/123RF; 70 (6): TinnaPong/Shutterstock; 71 (left): Beeboys/Shutterstock; 71 (right): Catalin Petolea/Shutterstock; 72 (spring): Olena Z/Shutterstock; 72 (summer): Lotus_studio/Shutterstock; 72 (fall): Dean Fikar/Shutterstock; 72 (winter): John A. Anderson/Shutterstock; 75: Selinofoto/Shutterstock; 76: rSnapshotPhotos/Shutterstock; 81(1): Kirill Kedrinski/123RF; 81(2): Maskot/Getty Images; 81 (3): Andriy Popov/123RF; 81(4): Hongqi Zhang/123RF; 81 (5): Elena Elisseeva/Shutterstock; 81 (6): Andriy Popov/123RF; 83: Cathy Yeulet/123RF.

Unit 5

Page 85: ColorBlind/The Image Bank/Getty Images; 86 (penny): B Brown/Shutterstock; 86 (nickel): B Brown/Shutterstock; 86 (dime): B Brown/Shutterstock; 86 (quarter): B Brown/Shutterstock; 86 (half dollar): Andrei Kuzmik/Shutterstock; 87 (penny): B Brown/Shutterstock; 87 (nickel): B Brown/Shutterstock; 87 (dime): B Brown/Shutterstock; 87 (quarter): B Brown/Shutterstock; 88 (one dollar): Onehundred Percent/Alamy Stock Photo; 88 (five dollars): Jonny White/Alamy Stock Photo; 88 (ten dollars): Onehundred Percent/Alamy Stock Photo; 88 (twenty dollars): Art-Studio/Alamy Stock Photo; 88 (fifty dollars): Onehundred Percent/Alamy Stock Photo; 88 (one hundred dollars): Pius Koller/ImageBROKER/Alamy Stock Photo; 89 (top, right): Original Photography by David Mager; 89 (one dollar): Onehundred Percent/Alamy Stock Photo; 89 (ten dollars): Onehundred Percent/Alamy Stock Photo; 89 (five dollars): Jonny White/Alamy Stock Photo; 89 (twenty dollars): Art-Studio/Alamy Stock Photo; 89 (fifty dollars): Onehundred Percent/Alamy Stock Photo; 90 (1): Jiri Hera/Shutterstock; 90 (2): Sergey Kolesnikov/123RF; 90 (3): Jane Waterbury/Shutterstock; 90 (4): Alexandr Vlassyuk/Shutterstock; 90 (5): Leah-Anne Thompson/Shutterstock; 90 (6): Jvart/123RF; 90 (7): Sergey Soldatov/123RF; 90 (8): Somchai Somsanitangkul/123RF; 90 (9): Mihalec/Shutterstock; 90 (10): Hurst Photo/Shutterstock; 90 (11): Murat Baysan/Shutterstock; 90 (12): Pixelrobot/123RF; 91: Iakov Filimonov/123RF; 93 (top): Dragon Images/Shutterstock; 93 (soap): Jiri Hera/Shutterstock; 93 (tissues): Pixelrobot/123RF; 93 (deodorant): Sergey Kolesnikov/123RF; 93 (light bulbs): Somchai Somsanitangkul/123RF; 93 (aspirin): Hurst Photo/Shutterstock; 93 (razors): Murat Baysan/Shutterstock; 99 (half dollar): Andrei Kuzmik/Shutterstock; 99 (penny): B Brown/Shutterstock; 99 (quarter): B Brown/Shutterstock; 99 (dime): B Brown/Shutterstock; 99 (nickel): B Brown/Shutterstock; 99 (one hundred dollars): Pius Koller/ImageBROKER/Alamy Stock Photo; 99 (fifty dollars): Onehundred Percent/Alamy Stock Photo; 99 (twenty dollars): Art-Studio/Alamy Stock Photo; 99 (ten dollars): Onehundred Percent/Alamy Stock Photo; 99 (five dollars): Jonny White/Alamy Stock Photo; 99 (one dollar): Onehundred Percent/Alamy Stock Photo; 101 (soap):Jiri Hera/Shutterstock; 101 (paper towels): Alexandr Vlassyuk/Shutterstock; 101 (shampoo): Mihalec/Shutterstock; 101 (light bulbs): Somchai Somsanitangkul/Shutterstock; 101 (toothpaste): Leah-Anne Thompson/Shutterstock; 101 (notebooks): Siraphol/123RF.

Unit 6

Page 103: Rawpixel.com/Shutterstock; 104 (1): Irochka/123RF; 104 (2): 5 second Studio/Shutterstock; 104 (3): Daniel Vincek/123RF; 104 (4):Tadeusz Wejkszo/123RF; 104 (5): Maria Dryfhout/123RF; 104 (6): Jiang Hongyan/Shutterstock; 104 (7): Geo Martinez/Shutterstock; 104 (8): Sergey Kolesnikov/123RF; 104 (9): Julija Sapic/123RF; 105 (top): Dmitriy Shironosov/123RF; 105 (center): Wavebreak Media Ltd/123RF; 105 (bottom): Iakov Filimonov/123RF; 106: Amble Design/Shutterstock; 107 (cucumber): Daniel Vincek/123RF; 107 (onions): Tadeusz Wejkszo/123RF; 107 (lettuce): Jiang Hongyan/123RF; 107 (peas): Julija Sapic/123RF; 107 (mushroom): Sergey Kolesnikov/123RF; 108 (1): Aneva/123RF; 108 (2): Oleg Vydyborets/123RF; 108 (3): Pushishdonhongsa/123RF; 108 (4): Paulo Leandro Souza de Vilela Pinto/123RF; 108 (5): Bryljaev/123RF; 108 (6): LianeM/Shutterstock; 108 (7): Provasilich/Shutterstock; 108 (8): Viktar Malyshchyts/123RF; 108 (9): Karramba Production/Shutterstock; 109: Sjenner13/123RF; 112 (bread): V.S.Anandhakrishna/Shutterstock; 112 (eggs): Stable/Shutterstock; 112 (chicken): Jiang Hongyan/Shutterstock; 112 (soup): Martin Bech/123RF; 112 (corn flakes): George Tsartsianidis/123RF; 112 (bananas): Viktar Malyshchyts/Shutterstock; 113 (top, left): Duplass/Shutterstock; 113 (top, right): Atic12/123RF; 113 (bottom, right): Blend Images/Shutterstock; 113 (bottom, left): Paulaphoto/Shutterstock; 114 (tuna sandwich): Gilberto Mevi/123RF; 114 (chicken sandwich): Liv Friis-larsen/Shutterstock; 114 (cheeseburger):

Foodandmore/123RF; 114 (baked potato): Olena Danileiko/123RF; 114 (green salad): Rafalstachura/123RF; 114 (fruit salad): Nataliia Kravchuk/123RF; 114 (french fries): Noophoto/Shutterstock; 114 (rice): MaraZe/Shutterstock; 114 (pancake): Hurst Photo/Shutterstock; 114 (eggs and toast): Belchonok/123RF; 114 (cereal): Jennifer Barrow/123RF; 114 (iced tea): Brent Hofacker/123RF; 114 (juice): VictoriaKh/Shutterstock; 114 (coffee): Pikselstock/Shutterstock; 114 (tea): Denis Larkin/Shutterstock; 119: Monticello/Shutterstock.

Unit 7

Page 123: Cathy Yeulet/123RF; 125: Primagefactory/123RF; 126 (sunny): Alexandre Zveiger/123RF; 126 (new): David Ronald Head/123RF; 126 (large): Katarzyna Bialasiewicz/123RF; 126 (small): Breadmaker/123RF; 128 (top, left): Trevorhirst/E+/Getty Images; 128 (top, center): Iriana88w/123RF; 128 (top, right): Glenn Young/Shutterstock; 128 (bottom, left): Interior Design/Shutterstock; 128 (bottom, center): Artazum/Shutterstock; 128 (bottom, right): Iriana88w/123RF; 131: Wavebreak Media Ltd/123RF; 137: Artazum/Shutterstock.

Unit 8

Page 141: TZIDO SUN/Shutterstock; 142 (1): Vetasster/Shutterstock; 142 (2): Karkas/Shutterstock; 142 (3): Tarzhanova/123RF; 142 (4): Windu/123RF; 142 (5): Nadezda Tsepaeva/Shutterstock; 142 (6): Ruslan Kudrin/Shutterstock; 142 (7): Karkas/Shutterstock; 142 (8): Olga Popova/Shutterstock; 142(9): Evikka/Shutterstock; 142 (10): Elnur/Shutterstock; 142 (11): Denis Rozhnovsky/Shutterstock; 143 (top, right): Mangostar/123RF; 143 (maxi dress): Tarzhanova/123RF; 143 (sneakers): Denis Rozhnovsky/Shutterstock; 143 (blue sweater): Ruslan Kudrin/Shutterstock; 143 (brown pants): Olga Popova/Shutterstock; 143 (grey skirt): Karkas/Shutterstock; 143 (jeans): Karkas/Shutterstock; 144 (center, right): Dmitry Kalinovsky/123RF; 144(t-shirt): Vetasster/Shutterstock; 144 (socks): Tarzhanova/Shutterstock; 144 (shirt): Nadezda Tsepaeva/Shutterstock; 144 (skirt): Karkas/Shutterstock; 144 (sweater): Ruslan Kudrin/Shutterstock; 144 (jeans): Karkas/Shutterstock; 150 (shirt): Karkas/Shutterstock; 150 (shoes): Heinteh/123RF; 150 (skirt): Karkas/Shutterstock; 150 (jeans): Elnur/Shutterstock; 150 (sweater): Karkas/Shutterstock; 150 (red jacket): Elenovsky/Shutterstock; 151 (sweater): Karina Bakalyan/Shutterstock; 151 (pants): Olga Popova/Shutterstock; 151 (grey t-shirt): Surrphoto/Shutterstock; 151 (shoes): Elnur/Shutterstock; 151 (sneakers): Nataliia Kravchuk/123RF; 151 (hooded jacket): Olga Popova/123RF; 156 (Jane): Maridav/Shutterstock; 156 (Vic): Wong Yu Liang/123RF; 156 (Tara): Jose Manuel Gelpi Diaz/123RF; 156 (Ken): Mark LaMoyne/Shutterstock; 156 (Amy): Javi_Indy/Shutterstock; 158 (Dress): Tarzhanova/Shutterstock; 158 (Jacket): Karkas/Shutterstock; 158 (skirt): Tarzhanova/Shutterstock; 158 (shoes): Heinteh/123RF; 158 (jeans): Elnur/Shutterstock; 158 (sneakers): Denis Rozhnovsky/Shutterstock.

Unit 9

Page 159: Thinkstock Images/Stockbyte/Getty Images; 160 (go online): Coleman Yuen/Pearson Education Asia Ltd; 160 (play the guitar): Hongqi Zhang/123RF; 160 (listen to music): Takayuki/Shutterstock; 160 (play soccer): Cathy Yeulet/123RF; 160 (exercise): Robert Kneschke/Shutterstock; 160 (watch TV): Prod-akszyn/Shutterstock; 160 (visit friends): Ferli/123RF; 160 (go to movies): Syda Productions/Shutterstock; 160 (play video games): Shutterstock; 161: Alessio Ponti/Shutterstock; 162 (left):Visuals Stock/Alamy Stock Photo; 162 (right): Oliveromg/Shutterstock; 163 (exercise): Pearson Education Australia Pty Ltd ; 163 (listen to music): Dolgachov/123RF; 163 (watch tv): Sirtravelalot/Shutterstock; 163(play soccer): Wavebreak Media Ltd/123RF; 164 (walk the dog): Moodboard/123RF; 164 (pay bills): Rocketclips, Inc./Shutterstock; 164 (talk on the phone): Shutterstock; 164 (do homework): Adrin Shamsudin/Shutterstock; 164 (wash the car): Volkovslava/Shutterstock; 164 (feed the cat): Littlekidmoment/Shutterstock; 166 (work on the computer): Burlingham/Shutterstock; 166 (help a customer): Dmitry Kalinovsky/123RF; 166 (take a break): Belchonok/123RF; 166 (take orders): Auremar/123RF; 166 (count money): Maryna Pleshkun/123RF; 166 (look for something): Wavebreak Media Ltd/123RF; 166 (answer the phone): Shutterstock; 166 (drive a truck): Robert Carner/123RF; 166 (fix cars): Antoniodiaz/Shutterstock; 167 (truck driver): Robert Carner/123RF; 167 (man counting money): Pisit.Namtasaeng.PS/Shutterstock; 167 (co-workers talking): Wavebreak Media Ltd/123RF; 167 (woman on phone): Dragon Images/Shutterstock; 168 (I'm late for work): Tidty/123RF; 168 (I'm sick): Auremar/123RF; 168 (I can't come to work today): Iakov Filimonov/123RF; 168 (bottom): Tele52/Shutterstock; 169: Tele52/Shutterstock; 173: Wavebreak Media Ltd/123RF; 174 (1): Siriphong Thumpharak/123RF; 174 (2): Andrey Kekyalyaynen/123RF; 174 (3): Wang Tom/123RF; 174 (4): Dragan Grkic/123RF; 174 (5): Sima Hui/123RF; 174 (6): Dolgachov/123RF; 176: Tele52/Shutterstock.

Unit 10

Page 177: Michaelpuche/Shutterstock; 178 (1): Hiya Images/Corbis/Getty Images; 178 (2): LEDOMSTOCK/Shutterstock; 178 (3): Daniil Peshkov/123RF; 178 (4): Shutterstock; 178 (5): Sandsun/Shutterstock; 178 (6): V J Matthew/Shutterstock; 178 (7): 06photo/Shutterstock; 178 (8): MIXA/SOURCENEXT/Alamy Stock Photo; 178 (9): Wizdata/Shutterstock; 180 (1): David R. Frazier/Danita Delimont Photography/Newscom; 180 (2): Glen Jones/Shutterstock; 180 (3): Ken Wolter/Shutterstock; 180 (4): Lim Yong Hian/Shutterstock; 180 (5): Bildagentur Zoonar GmbH/Shutterstock; 180 (6): Patrick baehl de Lescure/Shutterstock; 180 (7): Steve Heap/Shutterstock; 180 (8): Ellen Clark/Alamy Stock Photo; 180 (9): Cathy Yeulet/123RF; 182 (1): BraunS/E+/Getty Images; 182 (2): Martin Novak/Shutterstock; 182 (3): Tetra Images/Getty Images; 182 (4): Dean Drobot/123RF; 182 (5): Maskot/Getty Images; 182 (6): Luciano Leon/Alamy Stock Photo; 182 (7): Kristi Blokhin/Shutterstock; 182 (8): Leezsnow/iStock/Getty Images; 182 (9): Patti McConville/Alamy Stock Photo; 183: Apeloga AB/Cultura/Getty Images; 185: Iakov Filimonov/123RF; 186 (1): Sue Smith/Shutterstock; 186 (2): Robert J. Beyers II/Shutterstock; 186 (3, left): Steve Hamblin/Alamy Stock Photo; 186 (3, right): Steve Hamblin/Alamy Stock Photo; 186 (4): Creative icon styles/Shutterstock; 186(5): Georgios Kollidas/Shutterstock; 186 (6): Robert J. Beyers II/Shutterstock; 186 (7): Sue Smith/Shutterstock; 186 (8): Hank Shiffman/Shutterstock; 187 (stop sign): Sue Smith/Shutterstock; 187 (do not enter): Creative icon styles/Shutterstock; 187 (no parking): Georgios Kollidas/Shutterstock; 187 (speed limit 25): Hank Shiffman/Shutterstock; 187 (no u-turn): Robert J. Beyers II/Shutterstock; 187 (one way): Sue Smith/Shutterstock; 187 (no u-turn): Robert J. Beyers II/Shutterstock; 187 (walk): Steve Hamblin/Alamy Stock Photo; 187(don't walk): Steve Hamblin/Alamy Stock Photo; 187 (no parking): Georgios Kollidas/Shutterstock; 187 (stop): Sue Smith/Shutterstock; 187 (do not enter): Creative icon styles/Shutterstock; 187 (speed limit 25): Hank Shiffman/Shutterstock; 191 (1): Maskot/Getty Images; 191 (2): Allen.G/Shutterstock; 191 (3): Hugo Felix/123RF; 191 (4): Belchonock/123RF; 191 (5): BraunS/E+/Getty Images; 191 (6): Tommaso Altamura/123RF; 191 (7): Sheila Fitzgerald/Shutterstock; 191 (8): Leezsnow/iStock/Getty Images; 194 (1): SHUBIN.INFO/Shutterstock; 194 (2): PaylessImages/123RF; 194 (3): Janifest/123RF; 194 (4): Maximkabb/123RF; 94 (5): Alexander Oganezov/Shutterstock; 194 (6): Micha Weber/Shutterstock.

Unit 11

Page 195: Shutterstock; 196 (left): Ebtikar/Shutterstock; 196 (right): Ebtikar/Shutterstock; 197 (left): Belchonock/123RF; 197 (right): Manuel Faba Ortega/123RF; 199: Shutterstock; 201 (top, left): Nattanit Pumpuang/123RF; 201 (top, right): Subbotina Anna/Shutterstock; 201 (bottom, left): James Steidl/Shutterstock; 201 (bottom, right): MBI/Shutterstock; 209 (1): Viacheslav Iakobchuk/123RF; 209 (2): Mangostock/Shutterstock; 209 (3): Kurhan/Shutterstock; 211: Subbotina Anna/Shutterstock.

Unit 12

Page 213: Kali9/E+/Getty Images; 214 (1): Michaeljung/Shutterstock; 214 (2): Shutterstock; 214 (3): Michaeljung/Shutterstock; 214 (4): Steve Debenport/E+/Getty Images; 214 (5): Graham Oliver/123RF; 214 (6): Michaeljung/Shutterstock; 214 (7): Hongqi Zhang/123RF; 214 (8): Dean Drobot/Shutterstock; 214 (9): Dolgachov/123RF; 215: William Perugini/Shutterstock; 216 (1): Odua Images/Shutterstock ; 216 (2): PT Images/Shutterstock; 216 (3): Dmitry Kalinovsky/123RF; 216 (4): Hill Street Studios/DigitalVision/Getty Images; 216 (5): Rob Marmion/Shutterstock; 216 (6): Steven Vona/Shutterstock; 216 (7): PaylessImages/123RF; 216 (8): Nakamasa/Shutterstock; 216 (9): Andrey_Popov/Shutterstock; 218 (1): Koh sze kiat/Shutterstock; 218 (2): Jens Brüggemann/123RF; 218 (3): Ferli/123RF; 218 (4): Lucky Business/Shutterstock; 218 (5): Chutima Chaochaiya/Shutterstock; 218 (6): Sue Smith/Shutterstock; 218 (7): Andriy Popov/123RF; 218 (8): Dmitry Kalinovsky/Shutterstock; 218 (9): Cathy Yeulet/123RF; 219: Stockfour/Shutterstock; 220: Konstantin Pelikh/Shutterstock; 222 (1): Petervick167/123RF; 222 (2): Dzhafarov Eduard/Shutterstock; 222 (3): Vadim Guzhva/123RF; 222 (4): Michaeljung/Shutterstock; 222 (5): LightField Studios/Shutterstock; 222 (6): Scott Griessel/123RF.

Illustrations: Luis Briseno, pp. 130; Laurie Conley, pp. 33, 113, 147 (bottom), 148 (top), 149 (bottom), 155 (bottom), 198; Deborah Crowle, p. 6; Len Ebert represented by Ann Remen-Willis, pp. 16, 68, 86, 129, 148 (bottom); ElectraGraphics, pp. 18, 19, 22, 26, 37, 42, 46, 48, 49, 50, 60, 63-64, 76, 77, 80, 84, 94, 95, 98, 102, 110 (bottom), 118, 122, 124, 136, 146, 154, 172, 179, 181, 184, 185, 186 (#2, 4, 5, 6, 7, 8, 9), 188, 190, 192, 193, 202, 203, 208, 212, 226, 230; Peter Grau, pp. 20, 40, 58, 78, 96, 116, 134, 152, 170, 206, 224; Brian Hughes, pp. 110 (top), 111, 112, 144, 204; Luis Montiel, pp. 175; Roberto Sadi, pp. 34-35, 45, 125, 126, 139, 155 (top), 157; Neil Stewart/NSV Productions, pp. 72, 205; Meryl Treatner, pp. 147 (top), 164; Anna Veltfort, pp. 30, 36, 145, 149 (top), 200